JUMP INTO LEARNING

A Primary School Curriculum

REBECCA KRAUS ABBOTT

ISBN 978-1-68570-764-4 (paperback)
ISBN 978-1-68570-765-1 (digital)

Copyright © 2023 by Rebecca Kraus Abbott

All rights reserved. No part of this publication may be reproduced, distributed, or transmitted in any form or by any means, including photocopying, recording, or other electronic or mechanical methods without the prior written permission of the publisher. For permission requests, solicit the publisher via the address below.

Christian Faith Publishing
832 Park Avenue
Meadville, PA 16335
www.christianfaithpublishing.com

Printed in the United States of America

A collection of activities and poems to supplement the
social studies, language arts, science, and art programs.

User-friendly strategies that enhance each
child's learning experience.

This book is dedicated to caring parents who
equip their children with the learning skills necessary
for traveling through life's mountains and valleys.
Enjoy the adventure!

The Lessons in this Book Are Planned to Help You

1. Poetry has a significant role in childhood development. It's as important as music study in stimulating the learning section of the brain. It is also easier for the young child to enjoy and much easier than learning to play the piano.
2. The poems and activities in this collection cover a variety of subjects studied during the school year. Many color pages accompany the poems and lessons. The child will be involved in memorization, handwriting, art, science, reading, and story writing.
3. Detailed, user-friendly directions guide the teacher through each presentation.
4. The book is divided into monthly sections. A teacher may begin using this book to help the students anytime of the year. Labor Day, Thanksgiving, Christmas, Saint Patrick's Day, etc. have their own section of lessons.
5. Now is the time to begin making progress in scholastic achievement by using the strategies presented in this book.

Poetry used often in the classroom strengthens reading comprehension while also building the language skills of writing, listening, and speaking.

—Camille Hebert, reading specialist, Savannah, Georgia

The author was a teacher in the Kettering City Schools in Dayton, Ohio, for thirty years. During that time, she wrote many poems to use for handwriting lessons, memory work, social studies, science, and enjoyment.

Many of the vocabulary words are from the primary curriculum. Primary students will be able to read most of the material. The poems can be used for whole language teaching.

The poems are grouped in the order teachers would like to use them. The first poems are for use in August/September, when school begins. They cover self-esteem, colors, and the five senses, followed by seasons, weather, and activities that the children do during the holidays. The lessons continue through the year, including summer.

These poems and lesson plans are for the classroom teacher as well as the homeschool parent. The strategies can be used in many situations.

The author received her BA from Western College for Women in Oxford, Ohio, and completed several hours toward an MA degree at the University of Dayton and Wright State University. A class at Wright State for creative writing and the use of poetry in the elementary classroom inspired the author to write and use poems in her classroom.

Rebecca Kraus Abbott, Author

School Begins
August and September

Each child is special

"Each Child" is an introductory poem. It may be used with special children who have a variety of handicaps or in a regular classroom. This poem may be used to precede a health unit.

After reading the poem, children may be asked to describe their special ability, quality, and/or activity. The children could write about and/or draw themselves doing their best. Children could take turns naming their special talent, and, also, one special talent a friend has. This sharing among the class could continue until everyone has been noticed. Perhaps the children could find pictures of celebrities that have the same talents/handicaps and are successful.

Each child needs to know that he/she is a special and wonderful creation. The children need to realize that the teacher cares about their progress. This poem can help to convey these ideas to the students.

Include the family

Have the children include their parents, siblings, foster parents, or guardians. Each child can explain how his/her family is special. Each child can draw pictures, bring in photographs, create a family board, and/or write stories about special family events.

Each Child, All Children I

You are very special.

You are very grand.

You may be able to run very fast or

You may be able to use your hands.

You are a special person.

You know what you can do.

And it's because you're special…

I love you!

Activities and Discussion for Beginning School

Each of the following poems may be written on chart paper and hung to decorate the room for the opening of school. Perhaps the room could have a "Poetry Corner."

Labor Day

Discuss what Labor Day means, the history of the holiday, and the different ways people celebrate the day. Use pictures from the newspaper. Children may draw their own pictures. Write captions for their pictures. Write a journal about their activities.

First day of school

Discuss how students feel about the beginning of school. Ask them what they do to prepare for school. They need to be ready emotionally as well as having their supplies. Did they ever think teachers might have the same emotions? Draw a picture of one of the preparation activities. Put a caption under it. Display the class pictures.

It's important that students know their teachers like them. What about vice versa?

Studies for the year

Discuss what the students will learn during the year. Have them write/draw themselves doing these activities.

Weather in the fall

The weather is different in various parts of the country when school begins. Students can make a simple map and place the temperature in each weather zone. Perhaps groups of students could take sections of the country and follow the weather for a month. Compare the results. Students could collect pictures to display. Discuss how the climate determines how the children dress for school and how the buildings are built.

Ordinal numbers

Talk about first, second, third, etc. Have students line up with a sign bearing an ordinal number. Seated students can check their order. The words first, second, third, etc. can be used or 1st, 2nd, 3rd, etc. can be used or a combination of both. Students can match them. The months can be added.

Students may practice saying the months of the year. A discussion of the typical weather for that month can be included. Perhaps pictures for each month can be displayed. Numerals can be used to alphabetize the children's names. Use these numbers on their papers to place them in alphabetical order quickly. Have them line up by their numbers.

Weather art

Various items can be placed on the children's drawings. Spaghetti painted blue can be glued on the paper for rain. Cotton balls can be clouds. Pulled apart the cotton balls can be snow. Cotton balls can make a dandy snowman too.

The pictures can be made into a book for open house, the science table, and for enjoyment during Center Time.

Labor Day

Labor Day, a holiday,
A holiday of fun,
A parade in the morning,
A picnic in the afternoon.
We'll watch the bands,
Laugh at the clowns,
It's over way too soon!

School Begins

Summer's over when school begins.
I'm anxious to see all my friends.
Shopping for supplies is fun,
And I might get what I want before the day is done.
But then the first day is suddenly here…
I have mixed feelings of…CHEER…and FEAR!
I had trouble sleeping all through the night,
And now my hair is a dreadful sight!
I don't know where my books have gone,
And at recess, I stained my clothes on the lawn.

This day has been a big disaster!
I think I'll quit in the first semester.
But then a student says, "I love you."
And my heart melts. "I love you too."

Hello to Students

Hello to all of you coming to school.
You all look great and ready for the year.
Exciting studies are planned just for you.
You're sure to like it here.

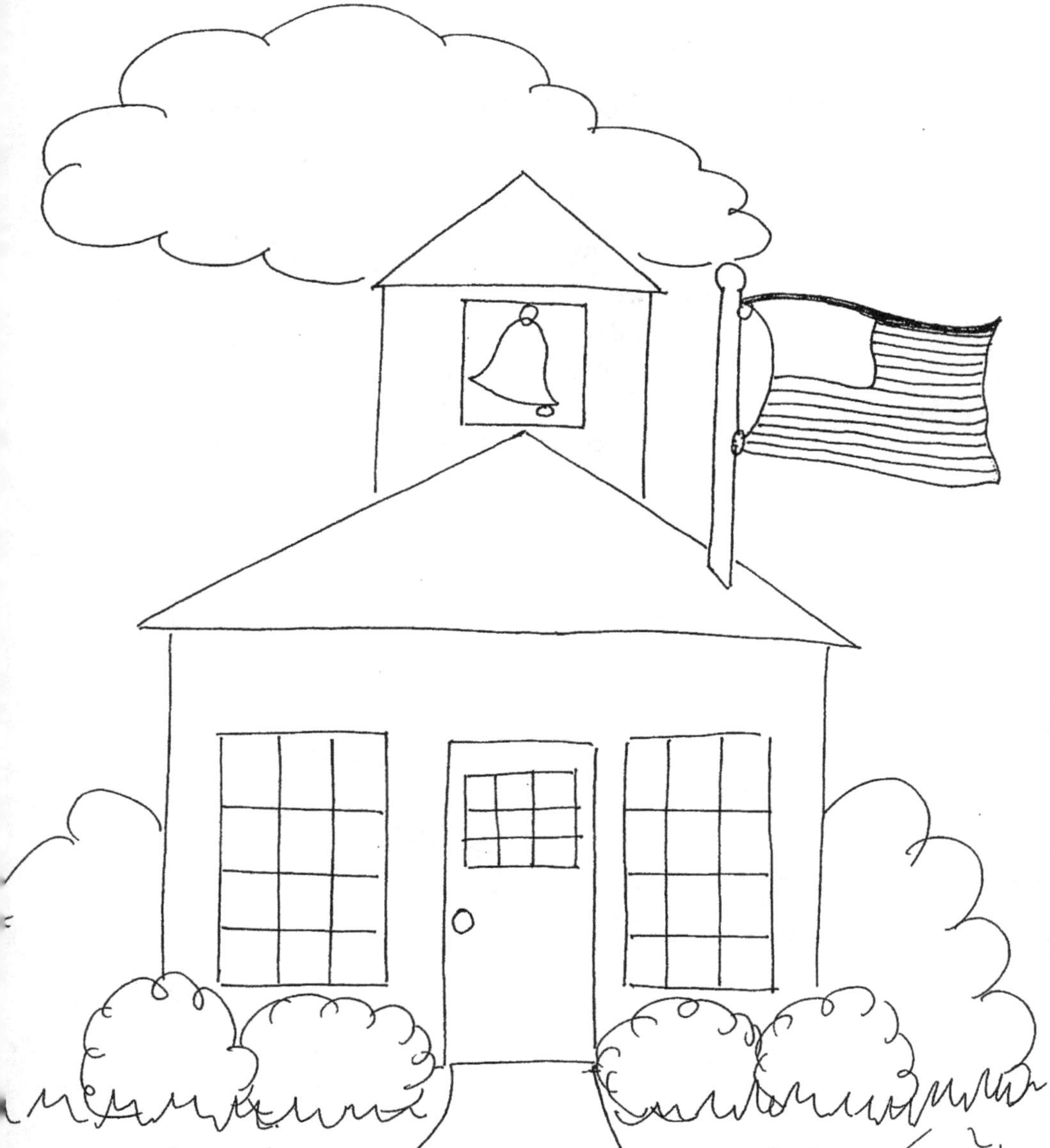
KRAUS

Welcome Back to School

Welcome back!
Welcome back to school!
The days will soon be shorter,
The days will soon be cool.
So welcome back.
Welcome back to school!

September Weather

September is the ninth month
That comes within the list.
Sometimes it's hot,
Sometimes it's cool,
Sometimes it's fog and mist.

When School Begins

When school begins, the weather's great!
The sun is bright and hot!
All I can think about is goin' swimmin'
And playing ball in the old lot!
But before too long, the weather changes
And it becomes real cool,
But let me tell you…
Recess is the only fun in school!

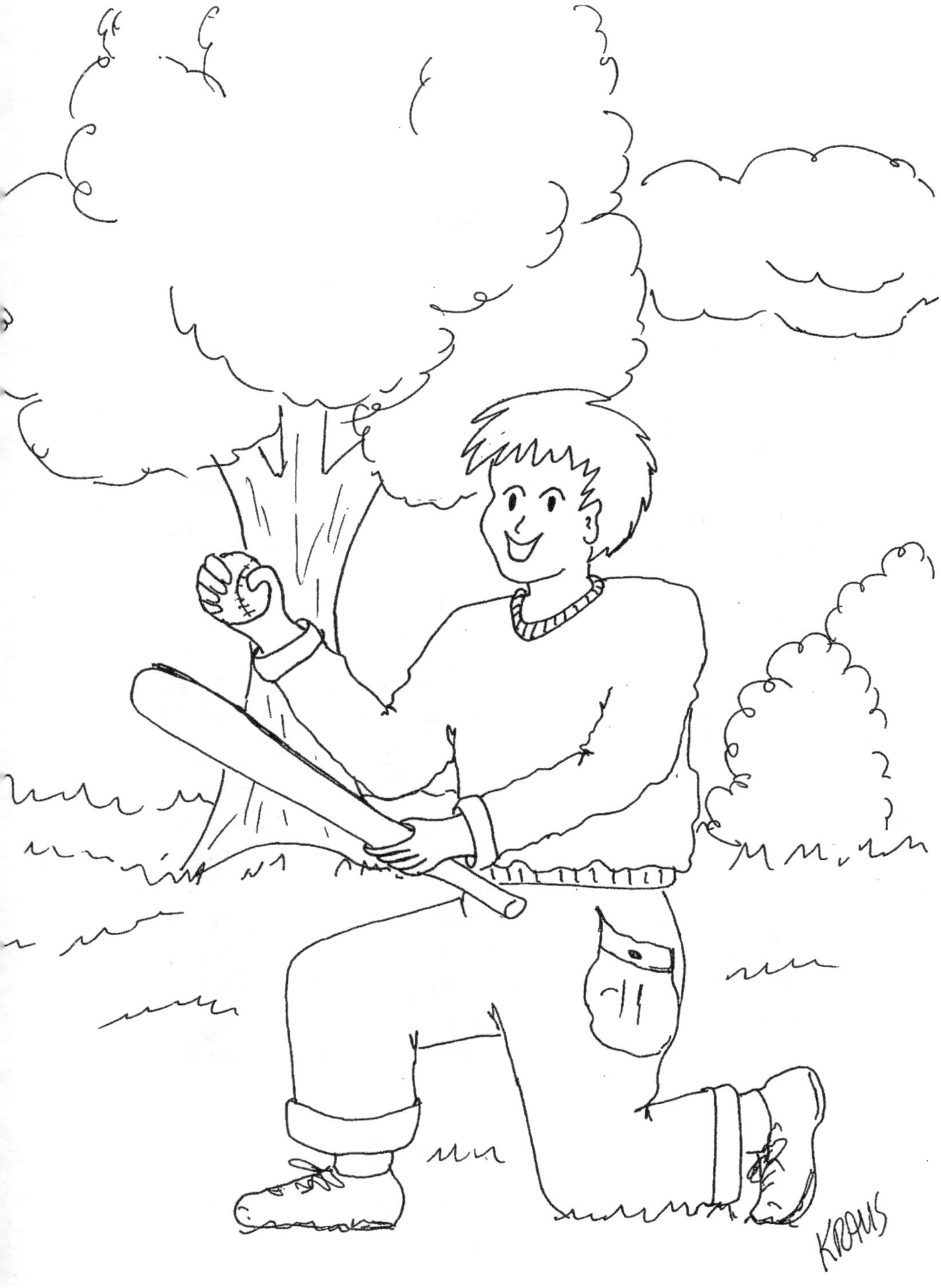
KRAUS

Colors

In the first grade, and even in pre-K, children learn colors and to read the color words.

The following poems can be used to help the children recognize the color words.

Read the selected poem with the class. Discuss the subject of the poem. Have the children color the color word in the poem with that color's crayon.

Activities to learn words

It helps to trace, write, spell out loud, and read the word. Use as many senses as you can to learn to recognize the word. These are called modalities.

Write the word on carpet squares with chalk. Have the children trace the word on the carpet pieces with their finger. They should spell the word as they are tracing it and read the word too.

Paste pieces of yarn on a paper to spell the word. Use red yarn for the word *red* or use red paper and red yarn. Trace the letters with the first finger and spell the word as it is traced. A book of color words can be made from these yarn papers. The book can be in a reading center.

A book of number words can be made the same way and placed in a reading center.

Lots of Colors

I see lots of colors in the sky.
I see white clouds go floating by.
I see blue birds flying high.
I love the colors in the sky.

I see lots of colors on the ground.
I see brown leaves that have fallen down.
I see orange pumpkins that are round.
There are lots of colors on the ground.

In my house are colors too.
I see yellow, red, and blue.
I see my green and purple shoe.
Yes, in my house are colors too

For Discussion

Ask the children if they can add other items to this list.

Red

Red is so very bold.
It's loud and full of power.
I like to use this color
And use it by the hour.

Red is also my favorite flavor.
It makes great cherry pie.
And it makes the world's best lollipops.
I think I'll give them both a try!

Blue

Blue is sad, blue is rest.
Blue is the sea at its best.
I love blue at night when I sleep
And enter into the quiet deep.

Orange

The color orange is happy and bright.
Orange leaves make a golden sight.
I like orange when it's my drink.
I'm glad it doesn't look like ink.

Brown

Brown is candy, the very best kind!
Yes, brown candy drives me out of my mind!
I like brown chocolate out of the box.
And I really like dark brown chocolate sauce.
That dark brown sauce over ice cream
Is so yummy, it's like a dream!
Yes, I surely would beg for more.
Please, Mommy! Let's go to the candy store!

Yellow

Let's think of things that are yellow.
Leaves in the fall are yellow, a candle flame,
A banana, a lemon, and a bag o' gold.
These are a few of the things I can name.

Yes, yellow is a color friend.
It's cheery and it's bright.
I like the color yellow.
It makes the world an awesome sight!

Green

Green is the color of a summer day.
Green is the color of springtime hay.
Under the shading leaves I play.
I could enjoy green all day.

Angelfish

In orange and purple, colors so bright,
A fancy fish would feel just right.
With these colors that truly shine,
It's the angelfish that looks so fine!

More Suggestions

The children may find pictures in magazines, cut them out, and paste them on a color board. Put the red pictures on the "Red Board," blue on the "Blue Board," etc. Large pictures from a coloring book can be labeled a certain color for the children to trace the color word and color the picture. A list of words can be under the picture; an example list: *one red, two red, three red, etc*. The children are to put a red ring around the word *red*. This can be repeated for all the color and number words.

Teach the children to color correctly. Trace the outline of the picture, then color inside the lines. Show them how to hold the crayon and the pencil. Follow the guidelines for making the letters correctly when they trace the letters. This is the beginning of good penmanship.

Remember to pull all lines down and start the circles at the top.

Name _____ Date _____

Red   red

Red   red

red	bed	road	red
was	red	had	mat
two	red	red	rid
red	see	red	red

Birds of Different Colors

Inspired by Spencer Jones, Age 4, February 24, 1996

Green is the hummingbird.
He flies around real fast.
And if you blink your eyes
He will have flown right past.

Black is the blackbird.
He likes to show his power.
He struts across the yard.
He does this by the hour.

Yellow is the oriole.
He nibbles my marigold.
He looks simply beautiful.
He's wondrous to behold.

Blue is the blue jay.
He likes to fuss and fuss.
He tells everyone where to go.
He's not nice like us.

Brown is the robin.
He's such a cheery bird.
He sings a merry song
And sends out the good word.

I am the redbird.
On my head I have a crest.
It looks like a crown
Because I am the best!

Birds

The children may choose their favorite bird to draw. They may write a story about it (with your help if they are too young to write).

Science

The body parts of birds may be studied. Explain why different body parts look different on a variety of birds. The talons, the beaks, the feathers, and the legs can be discussed. Decide on a few local birds for your study so the students can actually see the birds. Take a walk around the neighborhood to look for birds. Keep a journal to write about their observations. Carry a camera to record your findings. These pictures can be displayed on the board.

Art

The children may enjoy making a bird piñata. Use balloons, strips of colored paper, and liquid starch. Decide on a large fat bird. Cover the balloon with the strips of colored paper that have been dampened in the liquid starch. Let the paper dry. When it is dry, prick the balloon with a pin.

Find a desirable twig/branch from the yard. Place it in a jar that will hold it. If the branch is small, put rice in the jar to secure it. If it is large, plaster may have to be used to secure it. A variety of bird pictures may be glued to the "tree." Leaves of the season may be added to the tree. Encourage correct shapes and sizes. Make the birds and leaves as close as possible to the actual leaf and bird.

The children may wish to make clay birds. They can make them from cornstarch clay. The directions are on the box. After the clay dries, the birds can be painted.

The children may finger paint birds and trees. Use a variety of colors. The purpose is to enjoy learning the color words. Label the jars with the color names and have the jars covered so the children will have to read to get the color they want.

Seasons

A study of the seasons is always a part of the elementary curriculum. Children learn the connection between the months of the year and their season. They should be aware of the three months for fall, winter, spring, and summer. Though the intensity of the weather varies from section to section of the country, each season does have its own characteristics. For this study, the typical yearly cycle is used.

Seasons

Fall is such an awful mess,
At least my parents think it is!
But me, I like to run and play
And jump in all the leaves!

Winter's such an awful mess,
At least my parents think it is!
But me, I like to run and slide
On all the ice there is!

Spring is such an awful mess,
At least my parents think it is!
But me, I like to jump in puddles
And splash up to my knees!

Summer is such an awful mess,
At least my parents think it is!
But me, I like my toes in dirt
And climbing all the trees!

Children may act out each season's joy. They may recite the repeating verses.

The class could do a choral reading. Half the class could be the parents, and the other half could be the child. The class could be split into four parts, each part reading one season. The children could draw pictures of one season and use that part of the poem for a caption. Parts of the poem could be used for a writing lesson. Have the children continue the idea for a creative writing lesson.

The children may enjoy a walk outside to observe and record what they see related to seasonal activity. They can see what the animals, birds, plants, and people are doing in fall, winter, and spring. Perhaps summer should be included, just to finish the year. Ask them which season is their favorite and why. Ask them how their parents really feel about the seasons. Their responses could be grouped, graphed, and compared for discussion.

The reason for the weather changes should be discussed.

Apples and Johnny Appleseed

Apples—a writing lesson

An apple is round.
An apple is fat.
An apple tastes good.
I'm glad about that!

Johnny Appleseed, the Apple Man

Years ago, before cars and TV,
Back when Ohio was "The West,"
Lived a young man, a little man,
Who, some say, by God was blest.

He had a love for people
And he loved his apples too.
He planted them all over
For his friends both old and new.

He was born in Leominster
In September 1774.
The Bible was his favorite book,
It says in legend and in lore.

When the US was just a babe,
When the frontier was all brand-new,
Homesteaders had to plant apple trees.
It was the law, that's what they knew.

And Johnny was their apple man.
He had trees for the pioneers.
They carried his seedlings everywhere.
They covered six frontiers.

Excited by the journey West,
Johnny left for parts unknown.
He took his baby trees, his Bible,
His cooking pot, and ventured out alone.

He made friends with the Indians.
He made the settlers glad.
He traveled simply through the land
Bringing news and the trees he had.

He walked barefoot, going everywhere.
He planted trees and sold his seeds,
And some he gave away,
Helping each man with his needs.

He died in 1845,
And was buried beneath the sod.
He lived his life, his best to do,
To love mankind and honor God.

Activity

Have the children do a map study for J. Appleseed. Yarn can be used to trace his steps. A discussion of early American history can be developed. It should also be mentioned that Tom Jefferson doubled the size of the country with the Louisiana Purchase.

A National Hero Was Born in September

Johnny Appleseed

John Chapman was born on September 26, 1774. This short poem was written in honor of his birthday and to thank him for his contribution to our country.

He did several important things for our young nation. He provided apple trees for the settlers, he brought the news from neighboring towns, and he helped double the size of the new United States of America.

He was born in Leominster, Massachusetts. His father served in the Continental Army during the Revolution. John was about nine years old when the British left New York.

He decided to go West in 1797. The law stated that people wishing to homestead in the West had to plant fifty acres to claim their land. Johnny provided their apple trees and seeds. He was there when he was needed. Everyone liked him and thanked him for his help.

The Story of Johnny Appleseed

John Chapman was his name.
The apple business was his game.
He was born in late September,
And as we can best remember,
He went West with his apple seeds,
To help the settlers with their needs.
He had his Bible and a pot,
But a gun he carried not.
He was a friend to all he knew,
And because of him our country grew.
He's now a part of our country's lore,
So thank him for the apples in the store.

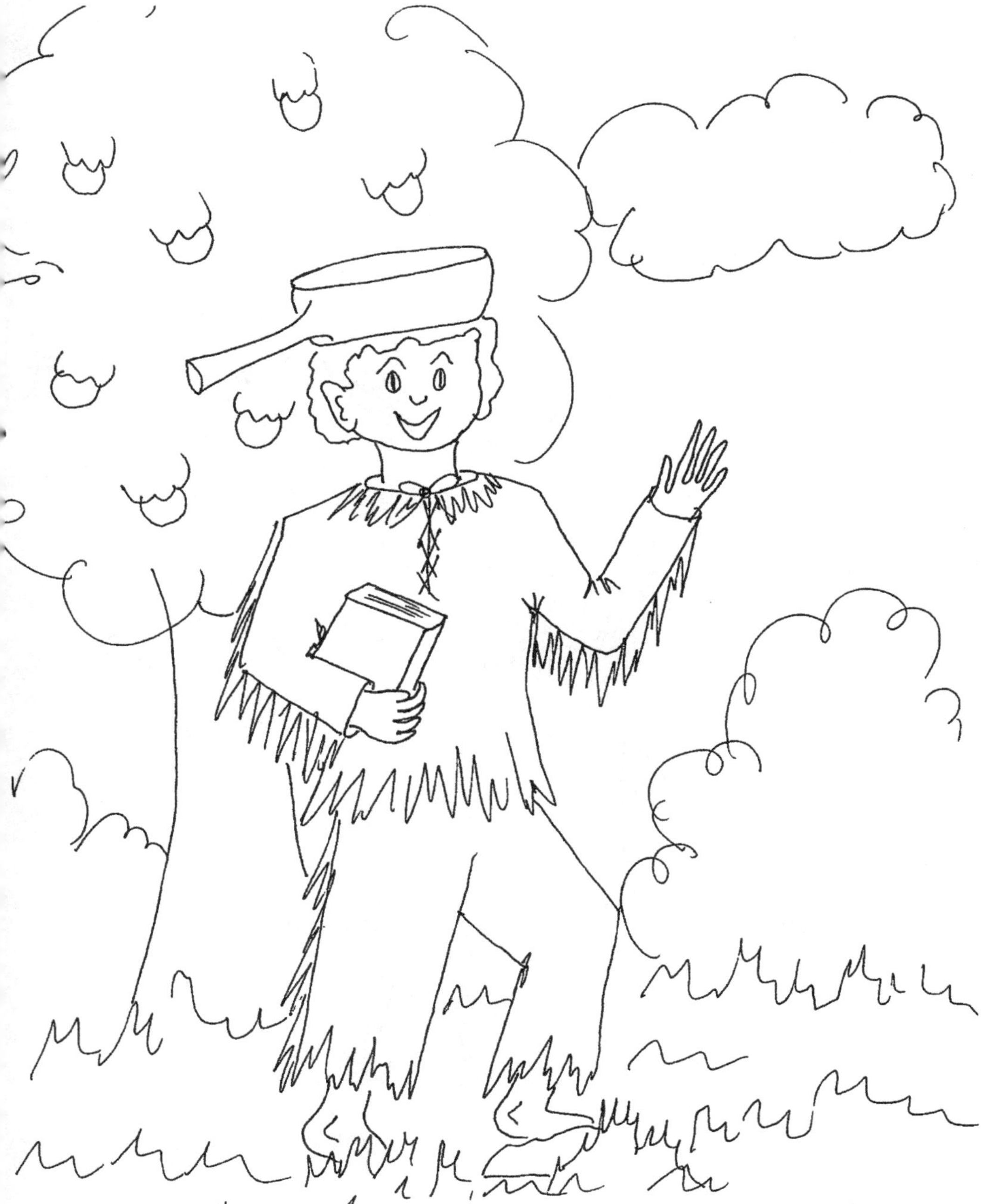
KRAUS

38

Activities for Johnny Appleseed

Make a list of all the things that are made from apples.

Children will enjoy making candy apples with the dipping caramel sauce from the grocery, and they will enjoy making applesauce in the microwave. Slice the apples. The skin can stay on and cook them until they are soft. Put them in a bowl with brown sugar and butter. Stir and serve. *Bon appétit.*

In 1948, Walt Disney produced a wonderful animated film about Johnny Appleseed. Perhaps you could find/order a copy from the Walt Disney Studios or it could be in a library. It has songs and a good story line. The children could learn to sing some of the songs. Slice apples crosswise to find the "star."

Try to describe the taste of an apple. Compare it to the taste of an orange, a strawberry, and a lemon.

Try to distinguish where the taste is on the tongue for various things: salt, apples, onions, and lemons. Make a diagram of the tongue and where these sensations are.

Discuss what was happening in the country during Johnny's lifetime. Who was famous? What was school like when Johnny was your age? What games did the children play? Rent a video or a CD that shows early frontier life.

Biography

Have the children imagine they are Johnny. Each child can write a short story about being Johnny Appleseed. Be sure to remind them to have (1) a beginning, (2) a middle, and (3) an end. Tell the children to illustrate their stories. They can share them with their classmates.

Teaching Shapes by Using them in Art

Circles

Apples with Johnny Appleseed

1. Cut two (2) round red shapes the same size.
2. Punch holes around the edges.
3. Stitch together with red yarn.
4. Stuff with a piece of newspaper or tissue.
5. Finish stitching.
6. Add a stem.

Apple trees

1. Cut a rectangle trunk from brown or black paper.
2. Put different shades of green ovals on top of the trunk.
3. Put round red circles on the green ovals. Dimes and pennies may be traced.
4. Glue the apples on the "leaves."
5. The entire tree may be glued on blue paper.
6. Green "w" shapes can be glued on for grass.

Birds

1. Decide on a bird.
2. Make a round circle shape for the bird.

3. Add wings, a tail, and a head.
4. Label the bird when you glue it to background paper.
5. Add feet.

Rectangles and Triangles

Schoolhouse

1. Cut rectangles and triangles to make an old-fashioned schoolhouse. Use appropriate sizes.
2. Add a bell.
3. May be glued to background paper.

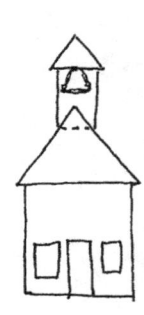

Ovals

Pumpkins

1. Cut orange ovals.
2. Stitch the orange ovals together with orange yarn.
3. Stuff with a piece of newspaper or tissue.
4. Add a stem.
5. If the children wish, they may add a face.

Ladybug—use with the ladybug nursery rhyme

1. Cut a very large red oval.
2. Punch two holes for the black pipe cleaner antennae.
3. Add six black ribbon legs.
4. Thumbprint oval spots.

Ladybug

Ladybug, ladybug is not a pest,
Lives in the garden in ladybug's nest.
Brings good luck to us they say
When she lands on me today.

About ladybugs

Ladybugs eat aphids, which are harmful to plants. You won't have to use insecticide, which kills bees. You can use ladybugs. Ladybugs are believed to be an answer to prayer. In the Middle Ages, the farmers prayed for help with their crops. The little red insect arrived and began eating the harmful aphids. They named the ladybug after the Virgin Mary.

Science Discussion

Insects and ladybugs.
Discuss characteristics of insects.
Three body parts.
Types of legs, purpose.
Four life stages.
Good and bad about insects.

October and November

The Autumn Months

Using the five senses

This is a good time to talk about adjectives—the describing word.

Talk about words that describe the taste of a variety of foods, not just fruits. Make a list of them. Graph them and group them. Maybe there is a class favorite.

Touch the fruit. How does the skin feel? How many different types of skin are there on fruit? These answers can be graphed too. How does the inside feel? Are fruits different from vegetables? What do the seeds feel like? Are the seeds different or alike?

If we put the seeds in a jar and shake them, we can hear them. The Indians put seeds in dried gourds to make rattles. Perhaps the class can do the same thing. They can make different rhythms with their rattles.

The children can also smell the fruit, put different fruits in brown bags. See if the children can identify the fruit from the smell. Try to think of words that describe the smell.

Apples Are for Tasting

I can smell the apple blossoms in the spring.
I can hear the bees buzz around them—ZING!
I can touch the smooth apple skin in the fall.
But when I taste it, that's best of all!

Popcorn

Our family went to visit the farm.
I walked so proudly on my father's arm.
We saw the cornstalks in a row.
The stalks were dry and crackled so.

We went to a table loaded with corn.
The kernels glistened on this chilly morn.
The Indians used corn in many ways.
Corn has been here for hundreds of days.

Now let me tell you what I know.
You can see the tassels with their golden glow.
You can feel the kernels; they're hard and round.
And when you pop them, they make a snapping sound.

Think of the hard kernels turned inside out.
They're white and puffy. Did you hear them SHOUT?
Yes, even the colorful Indian corn turns white.
Add butter and salt, and it tastes just right.

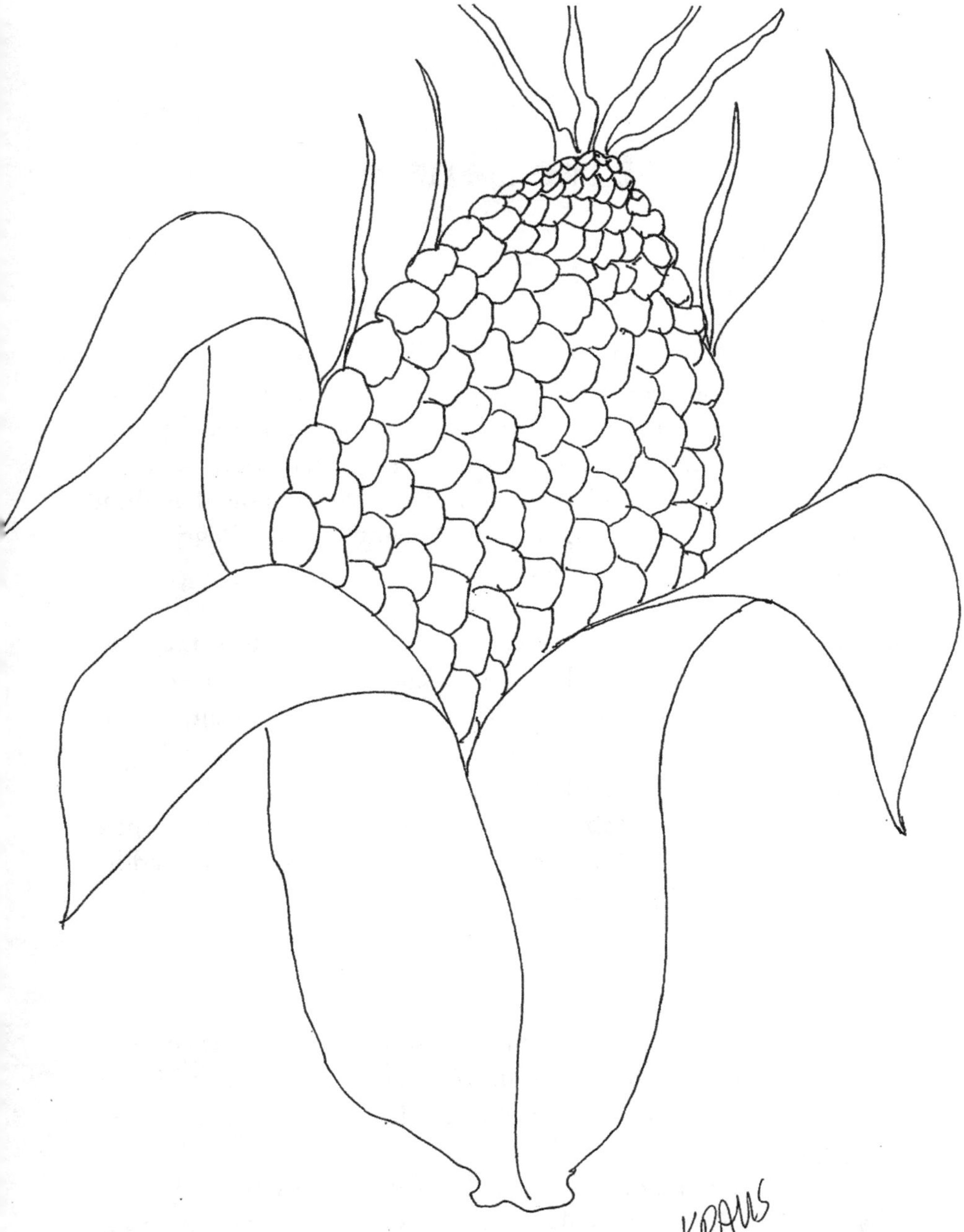
KRAUS

Five Senses

Popcorn

The popcorn poem can be used to introduce a history lesson about the Indians, perhaps Hiawatha and the Pilgrims and Squanto. Walt Disney produced a movie about Squanto that could be rented from the library. It has a PG rating if you need to know that ahead of time. There are several books about Squanto and the Pilgrims that are available on the primary level.

A discussion about farm life in America and farms in the fall could develop. Of course, the class should take a trip to the farm. Popping corn still on the cob can be purchased. The children can rub the kernels off the cobs, pop it, and eat it! Buy some cream too. Put the cream in baby food jars and have the children take turns shaking the cream to get the butter for the corn.

The class can write about their experience, including the emphasis on the five senses. Practice using sequence (beginning, middle, and end) and a main idea sentence for the story.

Art

The children can cut out a large skinny oval to be the corncob. They can paste corn kernels on it. Wrap green paper around it. Put tassels on the end. The tassels can be made from yellow floss or yellow paper.

Make a picture of the farm using natural pieces such as grass, leaves, twigs, stones, etc. Glue these items on paper, something like a mosaic. Tell the children how mosaics are made. Talk about how these items feel to the touch.

Science

Talk about plants, how they grow, and what they need to live. Put several lima beans inside jars with a damp paper towel around the inside of each jar. The children should be able to see the beans if they are between the paper towel and the glass of the jar. Be sure the beans will germinate! Watch the beans grow roots and leaves. If the children want to plant their sprouts in a paper cup, they may watch the beans grow into a tall plant.

Social studies

Talk about corn. Discuss its many uses. Corn is used for more than people food. Different varieties are used to feed farm animals and for fuel for the family car. Discuss the ways different cultures use corn. Talk about the ways the Indians prepared corn and compare those to the ways the Mexicans prepare corn. Plan a "dinner" for the class using corn in a variety of ways.

Fall Art and Other Activities

Pumpkins

The children can make pumpkins with brown lunch bags or with grocery bags. Stuff the bags with newspaper. Paint the bags orange. Tie the tops with green yarn. Add paper leaves.

Cut two identical pumpkins from orange paper. Punch holes in the pumpkin's rim. Stitch with orange yarn. Add paper leaves and a stem.

Trees

Trace the child's hand on different colors of construction paper. Be sure to use fall colors. Glue these hands to a tree trunk. Use the word *rectangle* to refer to the tree trunk. These trees will make great bulletin board trees.

Desk-sized trees can be made by using strips of curled paper for the leaves. Again, use the rectangle shape for the tree trunk.

Instead of curled paper, the children can use paper squares.

Landscape

The class may take their papers, pencils, and crayons outside to do a landscape picture. Another way of obtaining an outdoor picture is to have a photograph or a magazine picture to copy.

Still life

Have the children collect a variety of gourds and pumpkins. Make an arrangement of the vegetables where everyone can see them. Have the children sketch them and color their picture.

Science

Leaf identification

Do a study of leaf shapes. Leaves can be preserved by pressing them with a warm iron between sheets of wax paper. Be sure to use a cloth between the iron and the wax paper. Label the leaf collection.

Study the veins, the ridges, and the size of the leaves. Explain that the leaves change color because the leaf cannot make chlorophyll when the days are shorter. The chlorophyll makes the green color in the leaves. Use the Internet to find other facts about leaves.

Social Studies

Marking the winter solstice

Indians and other ancient people had to know when winter was coming. Somewhere near the village was a marker that the sun would hit to tell the people that winter was near. They may not have known about the equator, but they knew the sun was in a different place in the sky. Find some of these people on the Internet and the methods they used.

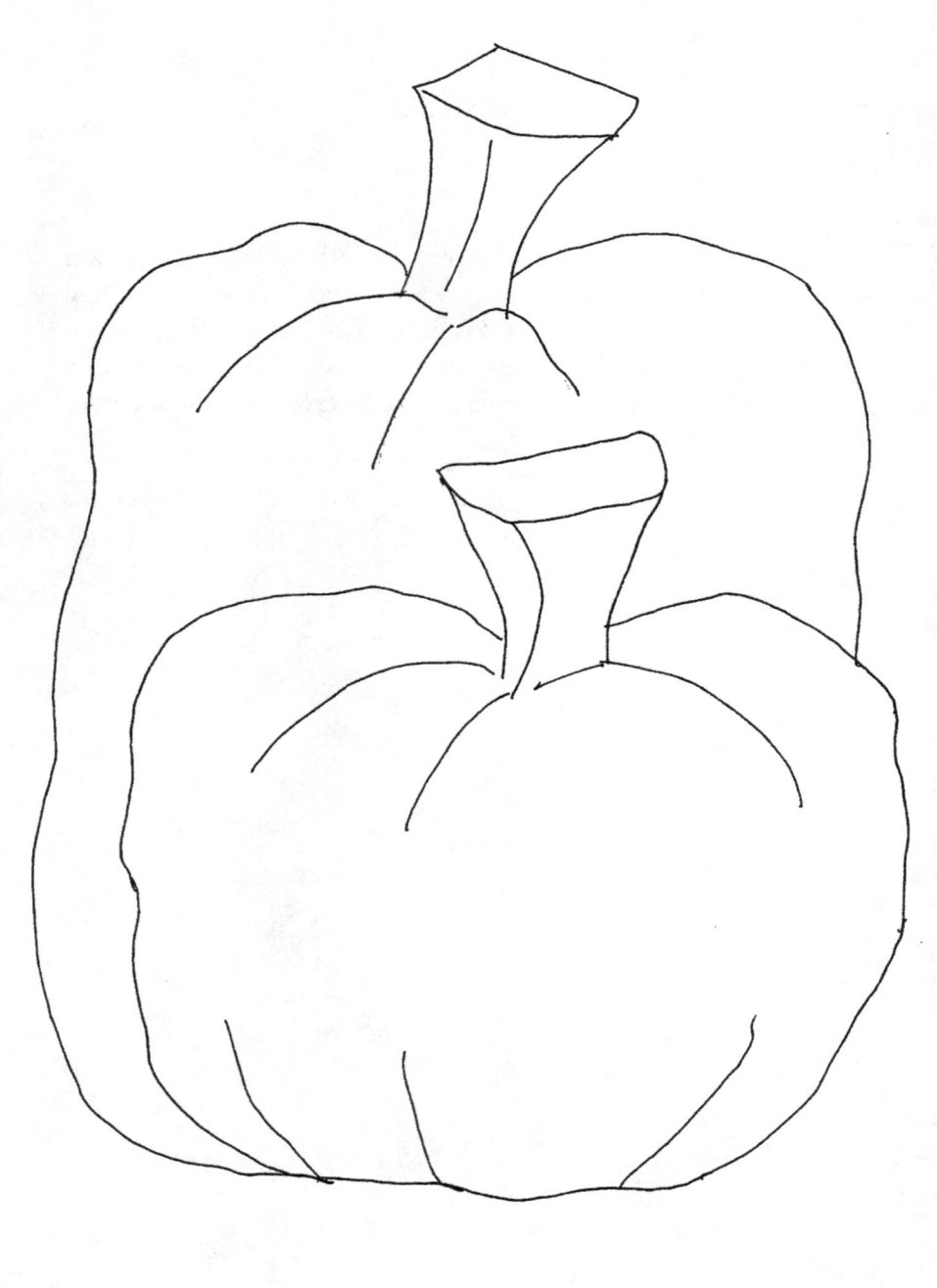

Poems for Use in the Fall for Handwriting Lessons

Pumpkins

Pumpkins are fat.
Pumpkins are around.
My pumpkin is the best pumpkin
That's ever been found.

Cats

Cats are soft, furry, and sweet.
They proudly march on quiet feet.
They can sleep while hardly stirring.
And when you pet them, they start purring!

Scarecrows

The old scarecrow is standing there.
On his face is one big grin.
The farmer thinks he scares the crows,
But he's made friends with them.

Maple Trees

Maple trees with leaves of gold
Are quite beautiful to behold.
All those trees standing there
Will all look old when they are bare!

A Walk through the Leaves

The crunchy leaves have their own smell.
The chill in the air has a lot to tell
About winter being on its way,
So let's enjoy this great fall day!

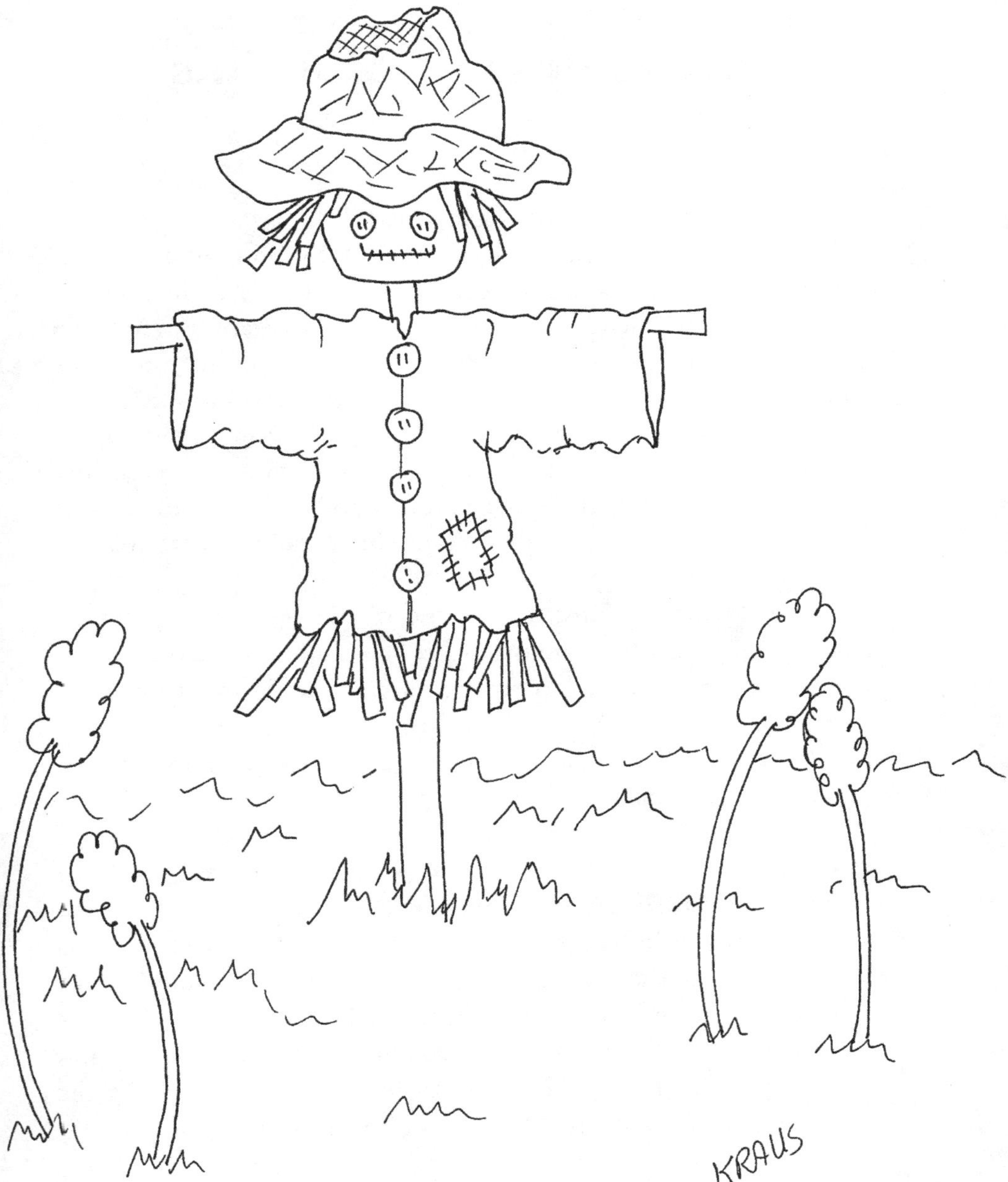
KRAUS

Christopher Columbus

So who was Christopher Columbus?

He was born in Genoa, Italy, in 1451. He was important. Many American towns are named for him. We celebrate his landing on San Salvador in 1492. School children study his explorations, and little ones make ships and study geography by following his route. His parents were weavers. Thus, he was in the working class. After his voyages, he was elevated in stature in Spain and became a member of the upper class. He was a poor sailor with an obvious gift for selling his ideas of a round world to the wealthy nobility. And from his conquests and discoveries (possible plundering?), he became a wealthy man.

We do owe Columbus. Because of his wonderful ability to advertise his plans for bringing riches to Spain and Christianity to the world, he was allowed to explore the Atlantic. These explorations won the interest of Europe. It was just a little more than a hundred years from the discovery of San Salvador to the settlement in Jamestown. A whole new era had begun.

Columbus can be viewed many ways. He was a brilliant navigator or he was just a lucky guy who bumped into a new world he thought was Cathay. He was a missionary to the natives or he was a villain for taking Indians to Spain as slaves. He introduced all those terrible germs to the Indians and thereby caused the death of many. He was a great governor of the islands or he was a leader that had to be recalled to Spain because he couldn't control his warring and greedy Spanish subjects. He even lost his distinction for being the first European to walk on American soil to Leif Erickson.

However you view Columbus, his discoveries will always mark the beginning of numerous voyages, conquests, and settlements, which eventually brought us to America. For all that, we owe Christopher Columbus a big THANK YOU!

Christopher Columbus—
the Poem

Born with an Italian name,
Cristoforo Columbo
Would one day achieve great fame.

He loved the boats, both old and new.
And watched their sails unfurl.
Someday, he would be a sailor too.

At fourteen years, he went to sea
To sail on many ships.
He was as happy as could be!

But, soon, misfortune played a role
And tore his ship apart.
He swam ashore, a young surviving soul.

He thought the world looked like a ball
And desired to sail its course.
And so on Ferdinand he would call.

Yes, bold Columbo went to Spain.
He promised the royal couple
Gold and silver and great gain.

In 1492, he captained his first ship.

It took longer than he imagined.
His angry sailors didn't like the trip!

Excitement soon would light each face.
"Land, ho!" the sailors cried!
San Salvador is what they named this place.

They claimed the land for Spain and God.
They seemed to settle in.
The first Europeans on this land to trod.

And with Spain's flag planted in the ground,
And prayers of thanks expressed,
Columbo had proved to all…the world is round!

Into history on his ship he went,
And left us with this truth,
It was Columbo that inspired others to be sent!

Columbus Activities

Social studies

Study the types of ships that were available in the 1400s. Compare them to the ships that were used by the Pilgrims. Compare their size to the ocean liners that are used today. Study the time it took to travel and the navigation techniques the sailors used. Compare their technology to today's navigational technology.

Think about their travel accommodations and the food they had. Discover the storage space for gear and food. Compare their meager comforts to today's cruise ships. Find information on wind currents and the jet stream. Discuss its influence on where the ships landed. Find out about the west and east wind patterns. The Gulf Stream also influenced where the ships went.

Find other books that explain the hardships of travel in the 1400s. The children will be able to internalize this voyage if they realize the reality of the trip.

Find pictures of the Indians Columbus found on San Salvador. Compare them to the Indians Captain John Smith saw at Jamestown. Talk about their culture. There's about a hundred years between the settlement at San Salvador and the one at Jamestown. Talk about the way the Indians received their visitors.

The Spanish settled in St. Augustine, Florida, around 1510. Did the Indians bother them? Can you find any other trips the Spanish made to the New World? Who were the explorers? Why were the Europeans racing to the New World? What kinds of people were risking their lives to get here?

Are immigrants still coming for the same reasons?

Why were the sailors scared of drowning? Of starving? Why did they fight among themselves? People fight today when they are scared of dying, starving, losing money, and/or feeling hopeless. What are possible solutions for these problems?

Have students pretend they are the sailors. Write about it. Draw pictures. Share. Write a short play to explain Christopher Columbus Day.

Turn a bookcase into the storage area for the Santa Maria. What items would be stored there? Include blankets and water. Discuss what items would be most important and why.

Use the chairs for bunk beds. A small table could be the galley. The children will gain an understanding of the voyage by pretending to sail to the New World.

Make a map of Europe, the Atlantic Ocean, and the New World. Use yarn to make a Travel line. Use different colors for each sailing. Put three small ships in the picture.

These are too many activities for one class. However, there are enough for different ages and abilities. Choose the ones that fit your group.

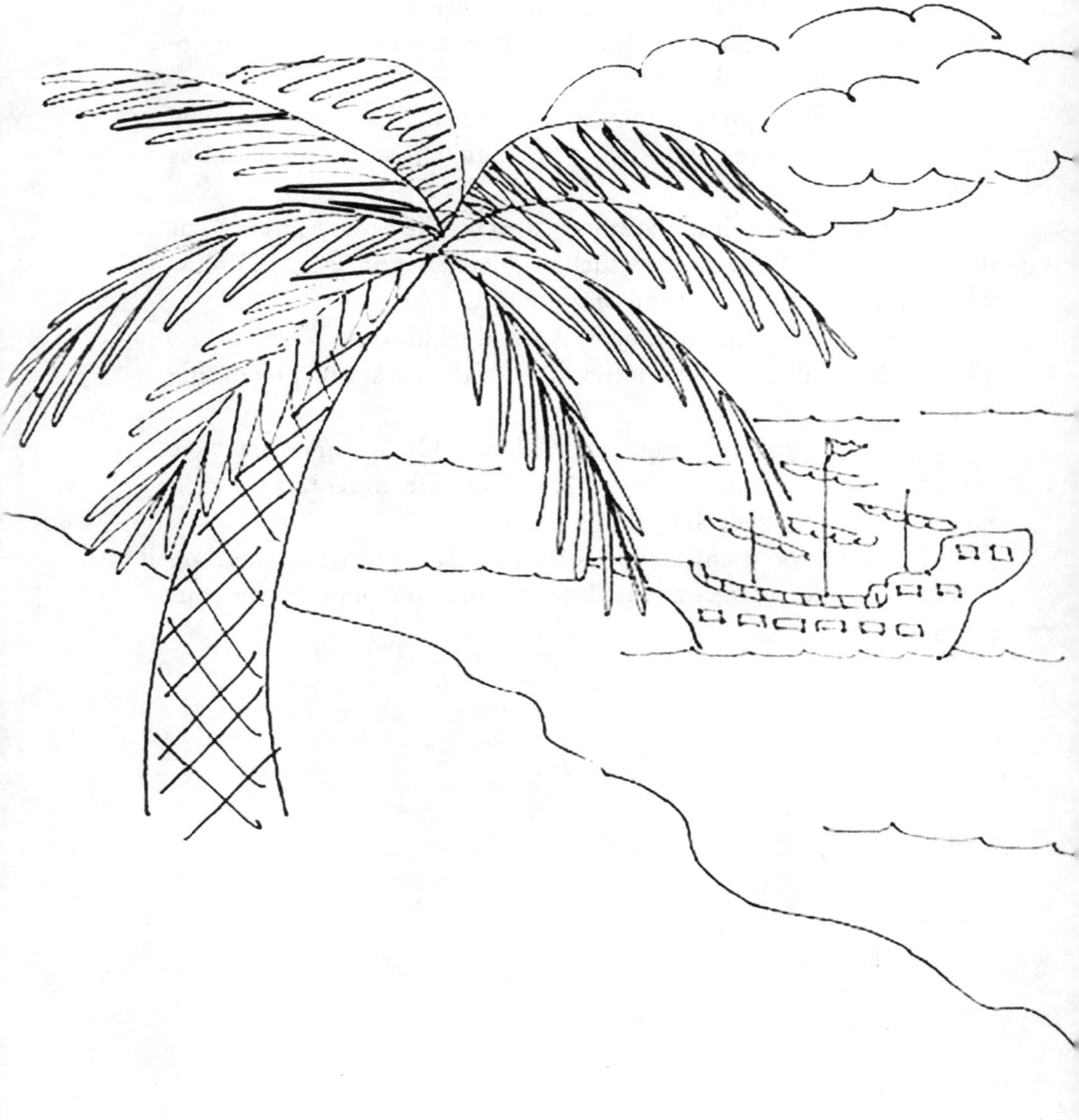

Halloween Lesson Plans

Plans that anyone can use.
Grandparents.
Parents.
Children can do it by themselves.

Strictly Halloween

Poems and Activities About Halloween to Enhance the
Language Arts, Social Studies, and Art Programs.

These Halloween poems are dedicated to everyone who enjoys the fun of dressing in disguise, collecting candy, and being thrilled by spooky decorations.

These poems relive the fun the baby boomers had in the '50s, before Halloween became a fearsome event.

So enjoy them. Imagine yourself back in time to a more peaceful era when Americans put God, family, and work first on their priority list.

Enjoy the adventure.

Poems About Halloween

The following poems may be used for handwriting lessons, discussion about trick or treat activities, choral reading, and/or to inspire a creative writing lesson.

Put one of them on chart paper to decorate the room, and the children will read it.

It is also a good time to study the human skeleton. Discuss the significance of bones and how to keep them healthy. The children can put a skeleton on black paper. Perhaps they can label a few of the bones.

Since this is a candy holiday, nutrition should be discussed. Since no one will stop eating candy, the children should know "the good, the bad, and the ugly" side of candy.

Halloween

Halloween is dress-up night.
It is the best night ever!
No one knows who I am.
It makes me feel big and clever!

Walking to the Neighbor's

I go up and down the street
Saying "Hi" to the friends I meet.
And I take my pillowcase
Over to the neighbor's place.
My dad and I watch out for cars
As I go begging for candy bars.
We are both having such a time.
Not doing this would be a crime!

The Haunted Street

The neighborhood is filled with ghosts!
I see dancing gypsies by the old gatepost!
And there goes a pirate with his skeleton crew!
(I hope I look scary too!)
Is that a bat behind me now?
And over there is a spotted cow!
The places that are usually all right
Are quite a fright on Halloween night!

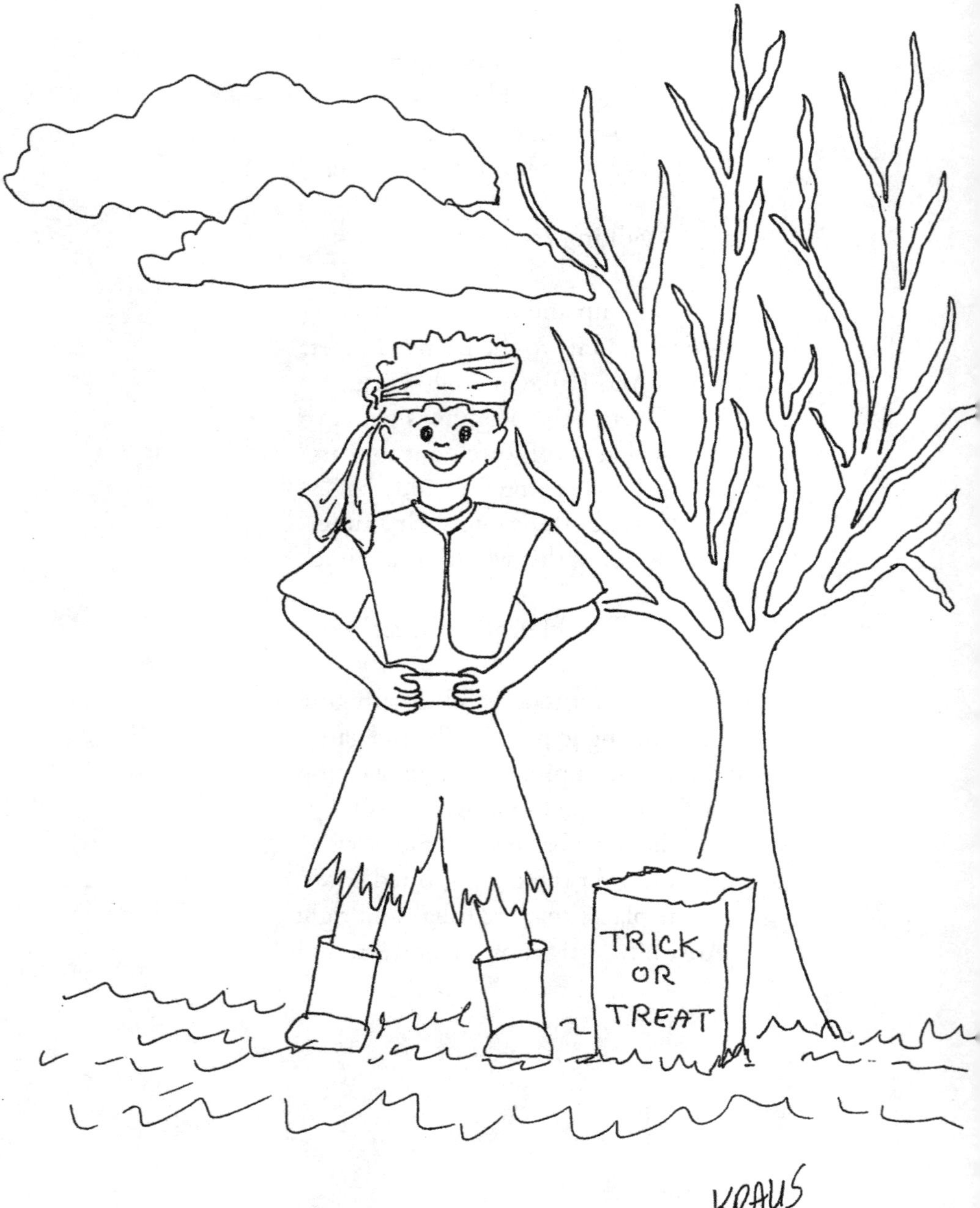
TRICK
OR
TREAT
KRAUS

Beggar's Night

Beggar's night is such delight!
It's so much fun for me!

I'll wear a mask and you will ask,
"Who's that behind my tree?"

I'll only say, "Your guess today!"
And "Thank you for the treat!"

Then I'll be gone as I go on
To the house across the street.

And when my sack upon my back
Is bursting at its seams,

It's home I'll go with a golden glow
Thinking of chocolate creams!

Yes, my chocolate prize seems giant-sized.
There's plenty here to share!

And it will last till Thanksgiving's past
And winter's in the air!

Trick or Treat

The night we go to trick or treat
Is really a lot of fun.
We see all our friends with their folks.
We're sorry when it's done.

Fall Activities to Go with Halloween

Use the short poems for writing lessons. Have the children find the rhyming words. Make lists of word families: *fun* followed by *sun, run, gun,* and *bun*; *treat* followed by *eat, seat, beat, cleat,* and *meat*. These are examples. You may use whatever you wish. A fall leaf collection can be placed on the science table. Leaves can be identified as maple, oak, redbud, etc.

Halloween (aka Beggar's Night) has a unique history. Bring in books that tell how Halloween began. It is from All Saint's Night or Hallowed Eve, but it has become All Haints Night. Have the children share their experiences about Halloween night.

Some children do not celebrate Halloween. Ask them to tell about it if they are willing to share. Have something for them to do. They may color pumpkins, make paper chains of brown and orange to use for Thanksgiving decorations, or write about their beliefs.

Haunted house

Read the story to the class, but do not read the last part. Let the class guess how the story ends. Then finish the poem. The children should have their own copy after you have read the poem to them. Have the children read the poem to themselves. After reading the poem, have them describe the house. Brainstorm for all the adjectives. List the words on the board. Maybe they could use the words to write sentences about the house. Maybe they could use these words in their own stories. Younger children can choose one word and draw a picture to go with it.

Questions:
1. Why is it a bad idea to go into a strange house?
2. What does the word *undaunted* mean?
3. What happened after they entered the house?
4. What were the scary things and why were they scary?
5. What were the normal things?
6. Why is the ending a surprise?
7. What are the *beginning, middle,* and *end*?
8. Name all the events that are included in the middle of the poem (the middle part tells all the problems).
9. When should 911 be used?

Have the children write their own haunted story. Children who do not wish to write a haunted story may write about other fall activities. These are raking leaves, going on a hayride, roasting hotdogs around a campfire, or stacking hay bales for a decoration in the front yard. Use a main idea sentence and the proper sequence.

Art

Cut out two identical bats. Punch holes in the outside edges. Sew them together with black yarn and stuff the bats with soft paper. Hang them from the ceiling.

Buy several yards of white muslin. Cut it into squares. Fray the edges. Secure a cotton ball in the middle with a small wire from an art store. Put pipe cleaners under the cloth and spread them out for arms. You have a classroom full of ghosts! A face may be painted on the ghost.

To make a really big jack-o'-lantern, use brown grocery bags, stuff them with newspaper, paint them orange, tie green strips of material to the tops, and add a face.

The Haunted House and the Old Man's Curse

The children entered the old house undaunted.
They had no idea the place was haunted.
It hadn't been lived in for several years,
And when the old man died, there were no tears
Because the old man had been so mean
To everyone he'd ever seen.

Now, just as Billy, Rose, and Sam came through the door,
It shut with a SLAM that scared them sore!
The place was dark, damp, and dusty.
Hinges on the doors and cupboards were rusty.
So everything squeaked and cracked
As they walked to the kitchen slowly, back-to-back,
So they could see in all directions.
They passed a mirror; saw their reflections…
And they saw the chandelier sway—
What made it swing that way?

It sang and hissed and hummed about,
Then turned itself on and turned itself out!
The children were speechless, scared to death.
They could hardly draw a breath.

When they entered the kitchen, a cold wind
blew chills across Sam's face.
They wished they had never thought of coming to this place!

But now they were stuck here for the night.
Perhaps for life if they died of fright!

In the kitchen, dusty cobwebs clung to their arms
While drawers opened and closed, giving cause for alarm!
Billy decided to go up the back stair,
As he groped in the dark, he could smell the bad air.
Rose and Sam followed, not knowing what to expect,
And then all three saw a sheet stand erect!

This whole idea of coming here was turning sour.
And it hadn't even approached the midnight hour.
A wolf could be heard howling at the moon—
If they could call 911, they'd all be home soon,
But alas and alack, they would have to stay here.
They would have to learn to live with their fear.
The howling wolf and the clouds passing the moon,
Let them know this would not be over real soon.

So down the hall to a bedroom they crept.
They went to the room where the old man had slept.
And just when they thought things could not get worse,
They opened the door and found a message
with the old man's curse,
Saying how he'd get the children, one by one,
And boil them into soup for fun!

Just then, from the walls came a blood-curdling laugh,
And an arm reached out to grab Billy's calf—

The children bolted out of the room and scampered
down the steps to the front door.

Then they rolled in laughter on the floor—
It sure is fun to pretend!

Other Haunted House Activities

Since the poem has no pictures, the children may want to illustrate their favorite part. Then they can put a caption with their pictures. The pictures can be put in sequence to retell the story. Have them share these pictures with the class. Three children at a time can share their part of the story.

Have them bring from home or the library other books about haunted houses, graveyards, and cities. Perhaps, if interest is high on this subject, videos from TV's *America's Most Haunted Places* program can be obtained. There's a lot of history learned from ghost stories. Ghost stories are in Savannah, Georgia, Williamsburg, Virginia, and San Diego, California. Maybe the children can find these stories and these cities.

Have them decide if they believe ghosts are real or not. Remember, this is all for fun. If it's too scary for them, don't do it.

A Few Halloween Poems for Handwriting Lessons

October Pumpkins

I saw many pumpkins on the farm.
They were round and orange and fat.
I found one that was perfect
For a jack-o'-lantern with his hat!

Ghosts

Ghosts are white.
They fly through the air.
But they're hard to see
Because there's nothing there!

Witches

Witches on broomsticks
Ride high in the sky.
They want to scare me,
I dare them to try!

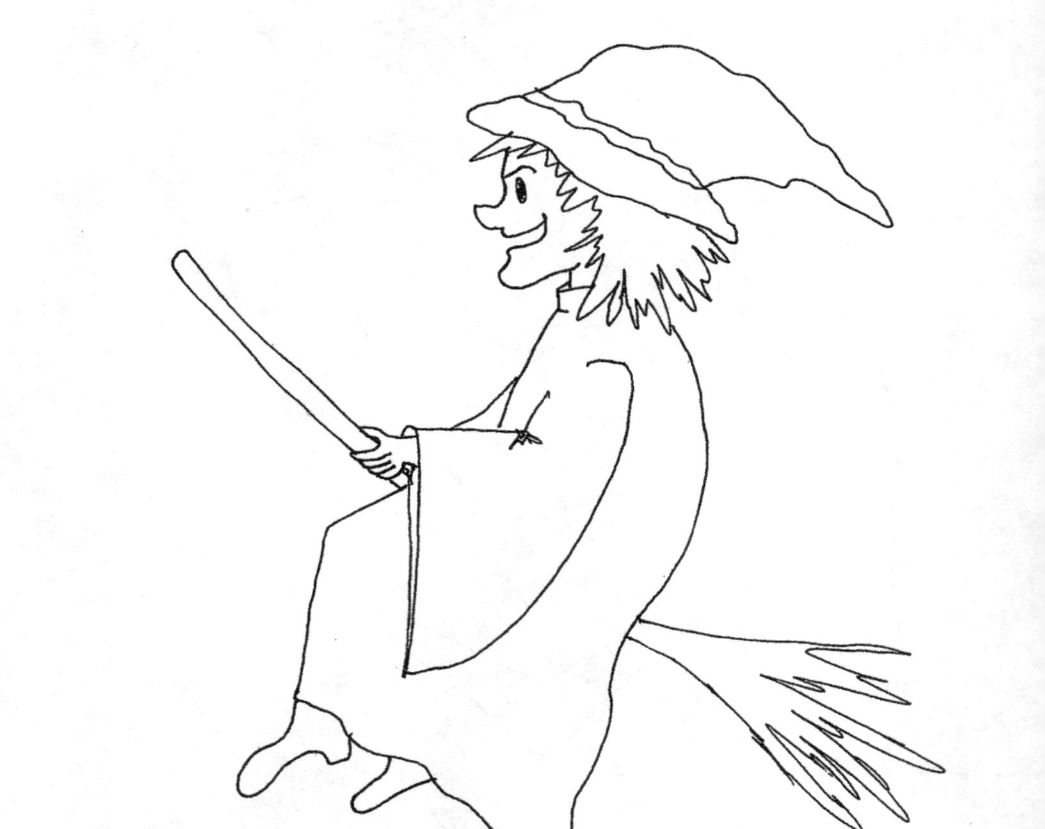
KRAUS

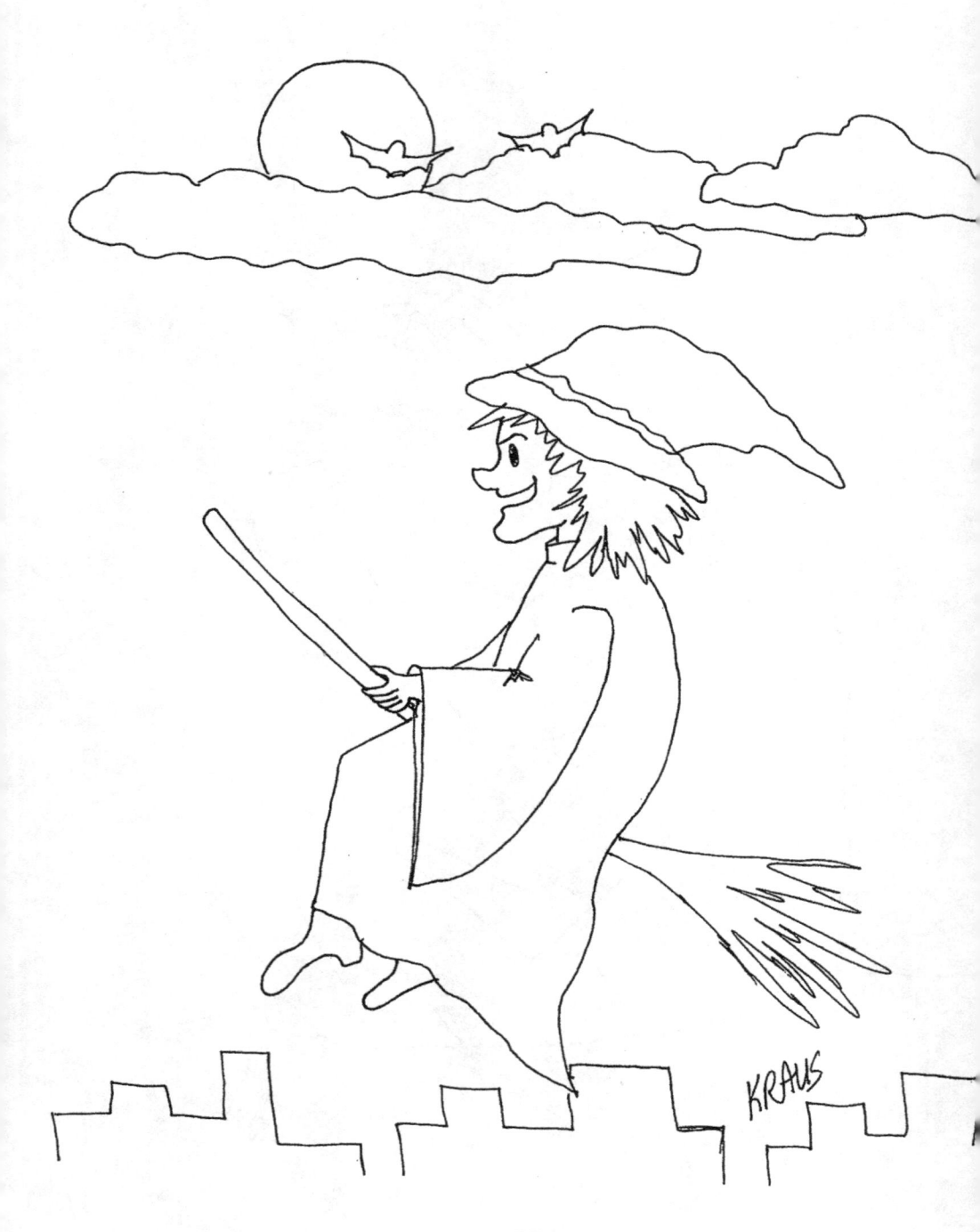

A Skeleton Just Clatters About

A skeleton just clatters about.
His bones rattle and click.
If he was not already dead,
He'd be so awfully sick!

Bats Fly but They Cannot See

Bats fly but they cannot see.
They don't know where they are.
They could be in a great big jam
If they didn't use their sonar!

Skulls and Crossbones

Skulls and crossbones warn of pirates
Traveling on the sea.
'Tis a symbol that danger lurks,
So it's careful you should be!

Tombstones

Tombstones are set in graveyards,
And they might seem to be quite scary.
They just tell us who's passed on,
It could be sweet Aunt Mary!

The Ghost that Lives in My House

I know there's a ghost living here.
He's an impish little man.
He likes to tease and laugh at us.
He takes our things when he can.

He hides in the laundry room
Where he must eat our socks.
He laughs and giggles
As he messes up our clocks.

I know I had a new hat right here.
And Jamie had a ball.
Jackson had a baseball mitt.
They're gone from the closet down the hall.

The keys used to be in the car,
Jamie's homework was by the door.
The icemaker used to work,
Now the ice flies all over the floor!

Yes, I know a teasing ghost lives right here!
He's taken it for his own.
And I doubt he'll ever move
'Cause he wouldn't leave us alone!

> We're too much fun
> When we're confused
> And can't find a thing!
> He's really quite amused!
> By all our wandering!

Some people would like to blame a teasing ghost for the items they misplaced. Perhaps a teasing ghost lives in your house. Draw a picture of your experience and write about it.

Fall Poems

October Feelings

The air is cool
And sometimes cold
In chilly October,
I've been told.

The leaves change color
From what I've seen.
They turn yellow and red,
They won't stay green.

Using poems for reading

The poems can be written on larger chart paper to highlight a season or holiday. The children can read them at their leisure. They help decorate the room with the studied subject matter. The teacher can ask the class questions which can be answered by reading the poem.

The following poem about rain can be used this way. It is written with primary vocabulary.

November Rain Poems

November is a rainy month in many states. It's convenient to have a few poems that talk about the weather and that the children can read. These poems could be at a reading center or at a science center. Keep the coloring pages with them.

The Big Surprise

Clifford Clown went out to play.
He went out on a sunny day.
Then the wind began to play.
And, soon, it was a rainy day.

My! What a surprise Clifford had!
The day became really bad.
But Clifford is a man that's glad
No matter the kind of day he's had.

So the wind will have its fun.
It will make Clifford jump and run.
It will do a lot before it's done.
The wind will have its fun!

When he put his umbrella high,
The wind blew Clifford to the sky!
He floated to earth with a sigh.
He sure is glad that he can't fly!

Clifford activities

Have the children find the rhyming words. Discuss the ending sounds and spellings.

Have the children contribute other words with the same sound and pattern.

Put the story in sequence. Talk about cause and effect.

Discuss Clifford's personality. What do they think would upset Clifford? Would he make a good pilot?

The Funny Day

The sun was out. It was in the sky.
The day was nice. The day was dry.

Then we had rain. And down it came.
It was wet. It was not the same.

Look at us! We're all wet.
Umbrellas up! And we're all set!

Then…the sun is here. Put your umbrella away.
Come on out. It's been a funny day.

1. What is the sequence? Beginning? Middle? End?
2. What did the person do to be all set?

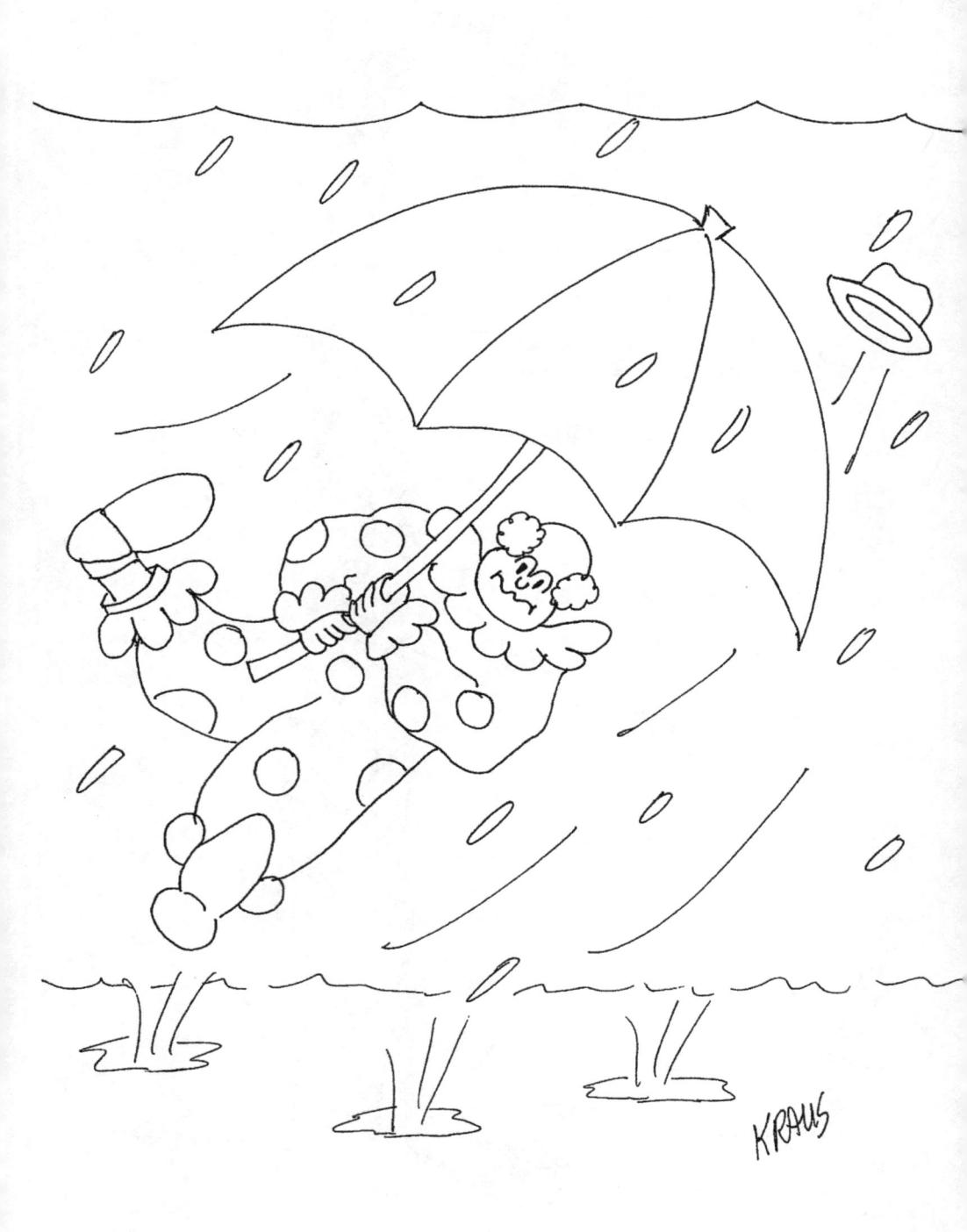
KRAUS

Rainy Days

Rainy days are really drab.
There's nothing much to do.
You can't go out to run and play.
You catch IT if you do!

So what's a person to do
When the weather is so bad?
I'll pretend I'm somewhere else,
And then I'll feel so glad!

I'll pretend I'm on the beach
And sitting on the sand.
I can pretend I see a shark
And be glad I'm on the land!

I'll pretend that I'm fishing
For a big old monster fish.
I'll tie some gum to a string
And catch anything I wish!

I'll pretend that I'm a pirate
Looking for buried gold.
I'll search the house for pennies
And all the coins I can hold!

I'll pretend that I'm a doctor
And operate on a doll.
I'll pull all the stuffing out,
Put it back, and have her standing tall!

Rainy days aren't so drab
If you pretend to have some fun.
It's really quite a super time,
But it's better when the rain is done!

Rainy Day Activities

Discuss the importance of pretending. What games did the child in the poem invent?

Have the class share games they have invented to keep themselves happy.

They may want to write about the game they invented and illustrate their story.

Take four verses and use them for a handwriting lesson. Have the children illustrate it.

Perhaps the class could write a short play about the poem. They could make puppets to perform their play. Puppets can be made from socks or paper lunch bags.

November Short Poems for Handwriting Lessons

November

November is quiet, still, and cold.
The trees are bare; they all look old.
There is no sun in a sky that's gray.
Oh, I wish it were a summer day.

Pilgrims

The Pilgrims came from England.
They came across the sea.
They braved the storms and crashing waves
To find their liberty.

Mayflower

The Mayflower was a little ship.
But it had a big job to do.
It carried all the Pilgrims to America
To start their lives anew.

King James

King James sat upon the throne.
He thought that he was grand.
But he was so very mean
That the Pilgrims left their land!

Pilgrim's Crossing

The sea was rough, the Pilgrims tough,
But, soon, they all had had enough of
splashing, crashing, smashing stuff!
When someone yelled, "Land ho!"
Off the ship they did go, into boats they had to
row, and, soon, their village began to grow!

More Thanksgiving Poems for Handwriting Lessons

Thanksgiving Dinner

Oh! What fun!
The turkey's done!
Let's pass the rolls
And eat the pie.
If I don't eat soon,
I think I'll die!

First Thanksgiving

The Indians came from far and near.
They brought turkeys, corn, and deer.
The Pilgrims fixed squash and apples sweet.
Everyone had a lot to eat!

November and the Pilgrims

Month of Pilgrims crossing the sea,
Coming to the *"Land of the Free."*
Oh, I'm glad they came for liberty
Which they gave to you and me!

Indians

The Indians loved their native land.
They loved the forests and the trees were grand.
While the deer roamed throughout the hills,
They fished the streams. It gave them thrills.
Our forests today are much the same.
Kentucky and Tennessee I can name.
We still have plenty of deer and lots of fish.
Our country has everything you wish.

Tom Turkey

Tom Turkey struts around the farm. He thinks he is so wise.
He doesn't know that, soon, he'll be sitting next to all those pies!

Activities

This is a good time to discuss the environment. Much of the land is the same because of state parks. There are still plenty of places to fish and hunt. The children could do a map study of state parks and recreation areas.

Find out which Indian tribes lived in your section of the country. Maybe there is a museum the class could visit.

Shopping for Thanksgiving Dinner

We're off to the grocery to plan our feast.
So we three kids get in the car…
And we haven't gone very far
When little Tommy screams out loud
And reports that Billy just hit him "for no good reason."

Mom turns around to tell us kids to button up
And keep those seat belts locked tight.
She says we need to shop tonight.
How she can talk to us and drive the car
Is a miracle! So far, we haven't crashed!

The parking lot is full of people, kids, and grocery carts.
We all get out of the car, eager to run!
Each one has a different place for fun!
Mom tells us nicely through gritted teeth,
To follow her into the store.

We know we have to behave now.
We can't wriggle, giggle, or act silly.
But then, we look at Billy.
He's juggling oranges and making faces.
This trip could be his last.

In fact, that's what Mom says

As she puts the salad into the cart.
Then she sees we've done our part,
We've helped pack the cart
By putting in a cake, some candy, and a pie.

"Well, if you really want to help,
You can find the things on this list."
She says while shaking her fist!
So off we go to find Thanksgiving dinner.
All of us are happy. This idea is great!

Back to the car we go, glad to be on our way.
Billy is playing a game with his feet,
And Tommy is finding things to eat.
We're looking forward to tomorrow…
No school, a TV parade, and a great big dinner!

Thanksgiving Day is certainly a WINNER!

Topics for discussion

Talk about the historical significance of Thanksgiving. Thanksgiving is celebrated in other countries on different dates. Abraham Lincoln decided to have a National Day of Thanksgiving to help the nation through the Civil War. Have the children do a little research to find other facts about the holiday.

Discuss the importance of the Pilgrims coming to America. Their lifestyle has had a lasting influence on our culture. Research their beliefs and form of government.

Activities

Make a list of all the things for which they're thankful.
Have them share the special way their family celebrates Thanksgiving.

A classroom may want to fix a small Thanksgiving dinner and pretend they are the Indians and Pilgrims. They can make simple costumes from construction paper. The girls can have white collars, and the boys can have black ones. The Indians can have feathers made of paper. If the dinner is a challenge, serve pumpkin cookies, apple slices, and popcorn.

Indian art

Use geometric shapes to make designs and patterns.

String beads to make a pattern.

Use Styrofoam meat plates (cleaned) from the grocery. Impress a picture on the smooth backside. Roll paint over the picture. The grooves should stay clear of the paint. Print the picture on brown paper (the inside of a grocery bag). This should look like a wood cut print.

Find Indian symbols in research books. Write these symbols on a piece of paper bag that has been cut to resemble an animal skin, then crinkle the paper and paint with very thin brown paint. It will look like an old Indian message.

Buy elastic from a fabric store. Measure the elastic to fit each child's head. Color the pieces with designs. Staple the ends to make a headband.

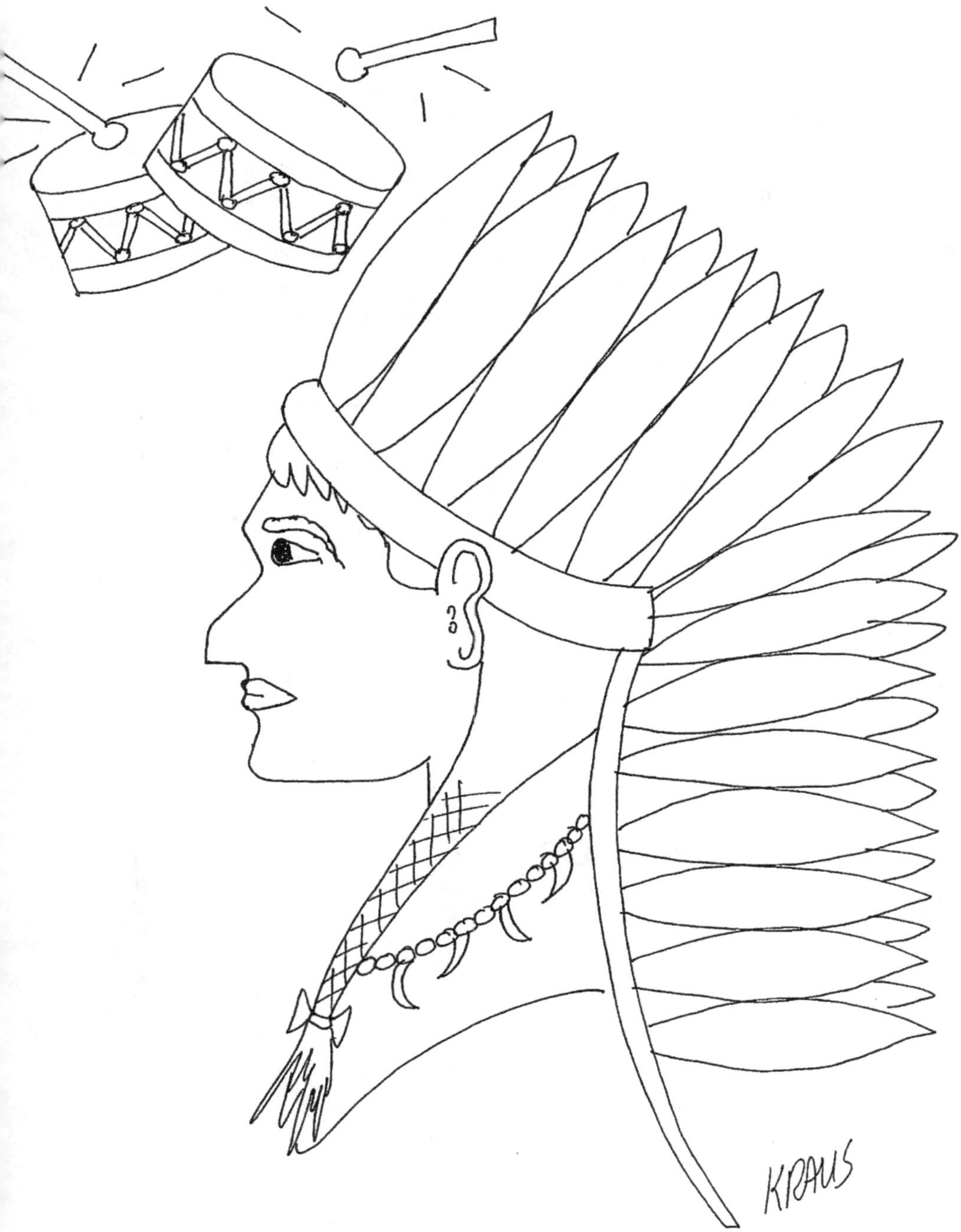
KRAUS

Pattern for animal skin.

Fold paper in half.
← fold

↓ fold

brown paper

December, January, February
The Winter Months

In some sections of our country, December is still quite warm, while in other parts, it is snowing! The poems in this collection will be about the snowy winter weather. Winter's woes of snow and ice are glamorized for the children who have never had the opportunity to go sledding, build a snowman, or ski down a hill. Those with these experiences may enjoy reading about these activities.

December is the month that Christmas is celebrated. It is the holiday of the majority. It is the traditional holiday. The poems and activities grouped in this collection are about the traditional Christmas.

You may include all the celebrations of this season in your studies. Hanukkah and Kwanzaa may be a part of your program. However, there are no poems on these celebrations in this collection.

The January section has poems about the snowy winter, Martin Luther King, Jr., and Rosa Parks. There is a poem about our nation's history and the immigrants.

The February section discusses politics, Valentine's Day, and the presidents, Washington and Lincoln.

The following poems may be used for display, general reading, handwriting lessons, and as "study starters" for topics that the teacher wants to teach.

Christmas

December is a happy time
When children sing,
And church bells chime,
When we share gifts with each friend
And pick out lots of cards
To send.

But best of all, we must recall
That Jesus was born
In Bethlehem's stall,
God's gift to save us all.

The last four lines are to be used at the teacher's discretion. The first six lines describe what most of America is doing. The last four lines describe a conservative belief system.
The next poem is on the same subject.
The poems following "Christmas Joy" are about the decorations with directions on how to make them for the classroom.

Christmas Joy

Joyful! Joyful!
We adore Thee as we sing our glad Noel!
'Tis our Savior's birth this morning,
That's the news we have to tell!

This is from "Ode to Joy" by Ludwig van Beethoven in 1824. Perhaps the class would like to see the original words and sing the song.

Candy Canes

Candy canes of white and red
Sparkle and dance around my bed.
While I sleep, it's all I see,
Candy canes are all around me.

Here they come and there they go,
Darting out into the snow.
Oh, I'm glad that they are gone
Or I would have eaten every one!

Holly

Holly is so pretty.
Its leaves are shiny green.
I think it adds a lot to the Merry Christmas scene!

Chains

Children make chains with colored paper,
Using colors of red, white, and green.
They add to the beauty of the room.
I think mine's the nicest I've ever seen!

Christmas Tree

Oh, how happy we will be
When we see the Christmas tree!
It looks neat with all the lights,
It's one of the season's prettiest sights!
And the way it sparkles so
Gives the room a special glow!
Yes, we love our Christmas tree.
I love the joy it brings to me!

Christmas Wreaths

Christmas wreaths of red and green
On doors and windows can be seen.
They are made from leaves of pine,
And from ribbon and some twine.
Some are sprayed with fuzzy snow
While others have an electric glow.
I'll hang a wreath made just by me!
It'll be the grandest you ever did see!

Lanterns

Lovely lanterns burning bright,
Glow and sparkle through the night.
Oh, they make a lovely sight
As they shine their soft clear light.
People who lived so long ago
Used lanterns to guide them through the snow.
They used a candle or gas streetlights
To guide them home on dark winter nights.

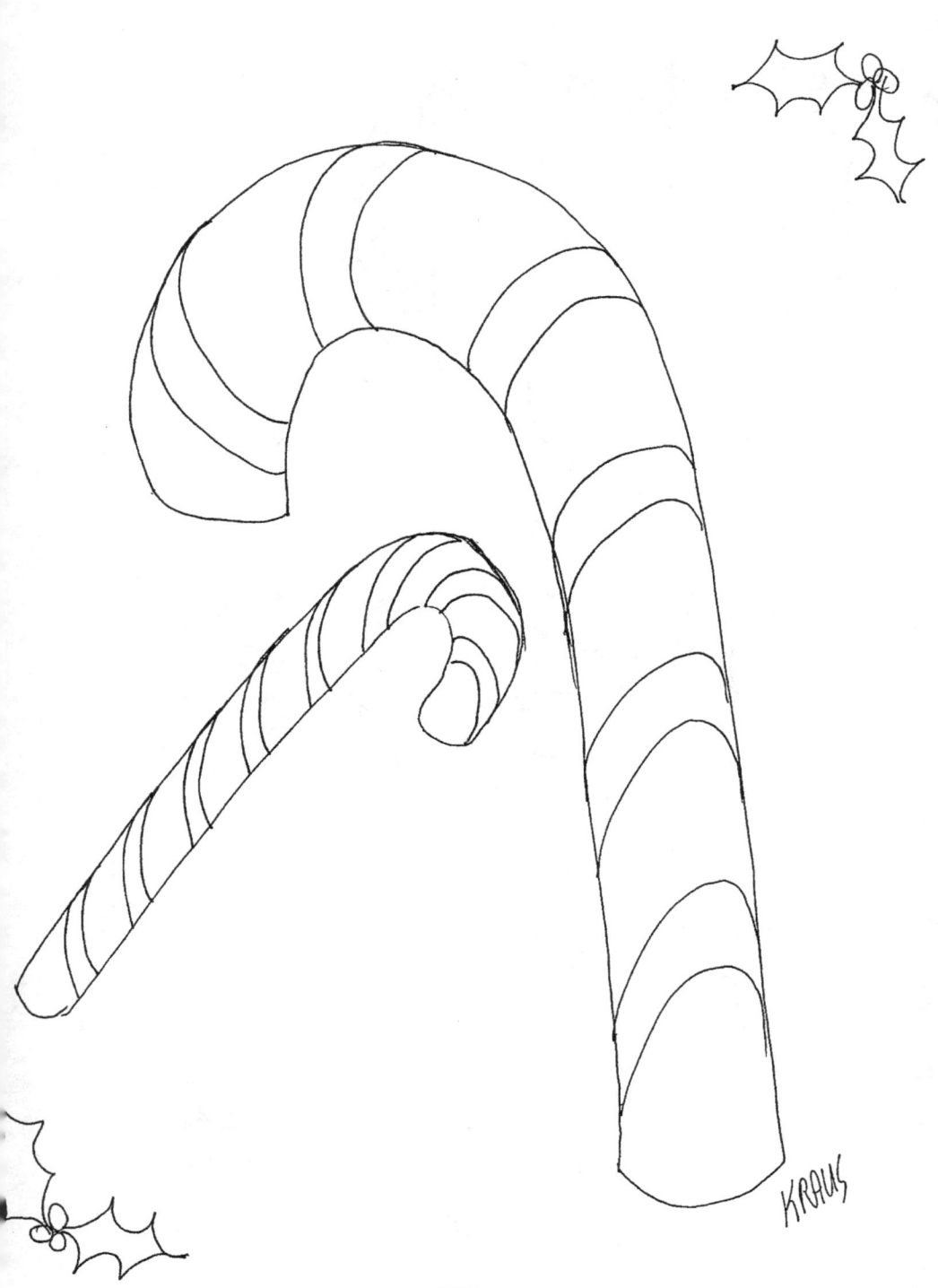

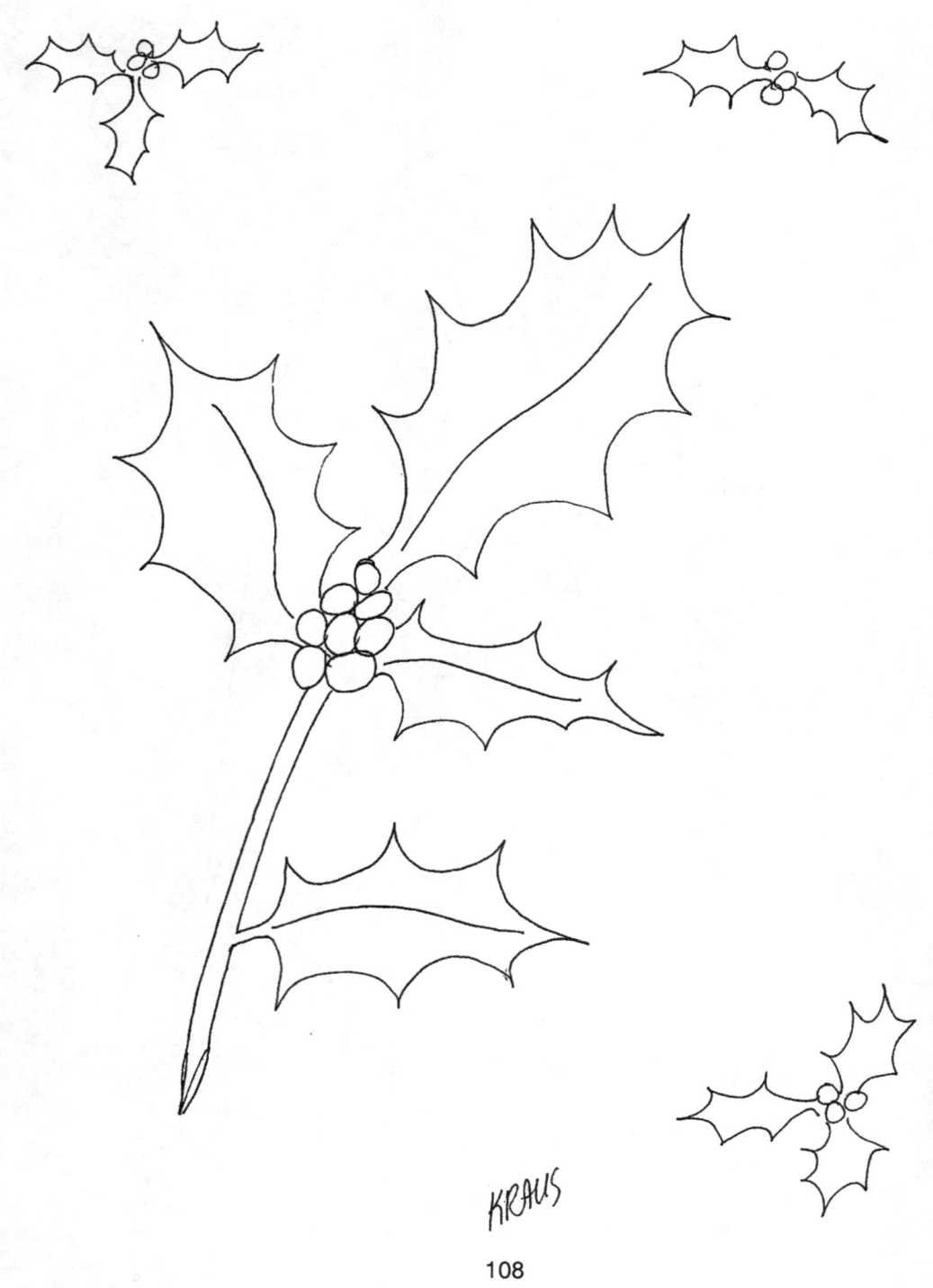

KRAUS

108

Christmas Art and Activities

Art

    Candy canes.
    Twist pipe cleaners to make candy canes.
    Use construction paper and glue.

Wreath

    Make an "O" on green construction paper. Cut small strips of green paper. Curl the paper strips and paste them on the O. Put a paper bow on the "wreath." Red paper berries can be added for color.

    The children may trace their hands on green paper. Cut out the hands. Glue the hands together to form a circle. Decorate the wreath with a bow, some berries, and bells.

Holly

    Use green pipe cleaners. Glue paper holly leaves on the pipe cleaners. The children may add red paper berries.

Christmas tree

    Have the children trace their hands on green construction paper. Cut out the hands. Glue the "branches" together to form a tree. This tree may be decorated with paper ornaments the children make. Small trees may be glued on legal-size paper, and large trees can make a bulletin board tree. Staple the hands together to make a desk tree that stands by itself.

Lanterns

Fold a piece of green paper in half. Cut slices from the folded edge of the paper, but not all the way through. Glue the ends together. A paper candle and a handle may be added. The lanterns can be hung from the ceiling.

Chains

Cut strips of paper the same size. Paste the ends together to make a chain. The children can make their own patterns. Be sure they understand what a pattern is. It's a repeated design.

Bells

Use yellow paper. Have the children draw two large bells. Cut them out and paste them together so that they overlap. Put a paper ribbon on them.

Reindeer

Have the children draw one small circle and one larger circle on brown paper. Cut them out and put the small circle on the larger one where a head would be. Add pipe cleaner antlers and brown paper legs. Of course, one can have a red nose!

I doubt you can find these clothespins today. Glue two wood clothespins together, add a wood ball for the head, and use pipe cleaners for the antlers. The children may draw a face on the ball with a Sharpie pen.

The Christmas Story—The Real Night before Christmas

The people in town were asleep in their beds,
But Mary and Joseph had no place for their heads.
They had traveled far to Bethlehem town,
And no inn for them could be found.

They saw one last place at the end of the street.
They slowly approached it on their tired feet.
They knocked at the door…
The innkeeper came…saw they were poor.

He said he had no room for them tonight.
But he looked at the couple in the dim lamplight,
And thought he might let them stay in the stable nearby.
And, shortly thereafter, he heard a baby's soft cry.

The angels were glad and flying about.
The heavens opened, and the sky seemed to shout!
This is my Son who is born today!
Praise God! And Jesus, he was just sleeping on the hay.

Now the shepherds who were in the Jerusalem hills,
Seeing the sky open just gave them the chills.
The angels told them to not be afraid.
They told them to go see where the baby was laid.

The shepherds were guided by the brilliant star.
They didn't have to travel very far.
And there in the straw with his dear baby face,
The shepherds saw Jesus, the Author of grace.

He had come to give people both hope and joy.
Faith and salvation were one in this Boy.
Now, as we prepare for a great Christmas season,
Let us be thankful as we note the reason.

God bless you all, and to all a good night.

January

Happy New Year
To one and all!
Come, be joyful
And have a ball!
It's time to begin
A fresh new start
Of resolutions and a willing heart!

Janu-Wary

January is
Ice and snow!
Cold winds that blow!
Cheeks with a rosy glow!
Cars skidding to-and-fro!
I wish January would quickly go!

Snowmen

Three little men on a hill
Are standing and smiling,
But they're stone-still.
Why are they standing out in the cold?
Why are they so white and so bold?
They are snowmen, and they're frozen cold!

My Own Snowman

My own snowman has a jolly smile.
He looks so glad and grand.
I gave him a broom to hold in his cold, white puffy hand.
He seems so proud out on the lawn.
He never has a frown.
But when the weather changes, his smile will be upside down!

New Hats and Mittens

Jim was happy with his new hat and mittens.
They were a birthday present for him.
He liked their nice bright colors.
He wanted to show them to Tim.

So over to Tim's house he went.
He was glad to have news to share.
He took his precious gifts with him.
But Tim was not there.

He found Tim outside in the snow.
He also had new mittens and a hat.
They looked just like Jim's new stuff.
They had a good laugh about that.

My Snowy Mountain

I live on top of a mountain.
We always have lots of snow.
I roll it into very big balls.
And I make snowmen. Some have a bow.

It's fun to live on the mountain.
I live where I see the sky.
I can see the other mountains.
And I see the animals pass by.

> The sun is always shining
> Where I live in the west.
> I always enjoy the bright, white snow.
> I think my mountain is the best!

Have the children discuss if they ever shared their presents with their friends like Tim and Jim did in the poem. What was the surprise for the boys?

Explain to the children that the Rocky Mountains have lots of snow and sunshine. Do a map study. Find other mountain ranges in the West that could be where this person lives.

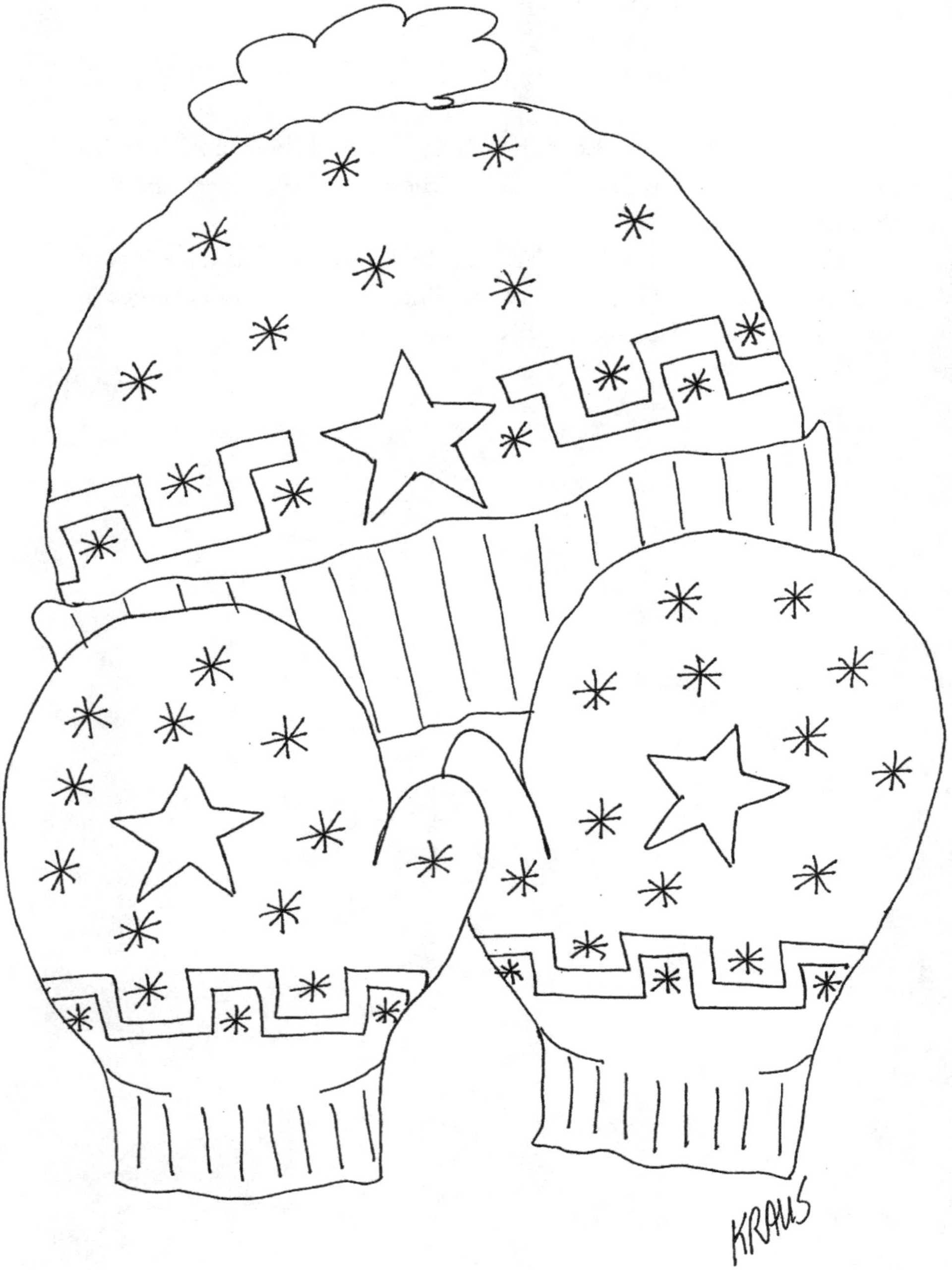
KRAUS

Sledding

What fun to go up the mountain!
I can see both far and wide.
It's fun to go up the mountain
And sled down the mountainside.

When I reach the top, I'm happy!
The view is great and grand.
I know I can race down the hill
And beat the best sled in the land!

I have a good time on the mountain.
I have fun everywhere I go.
I enjoy the sledding and the climbing.
I love it when there's snow!

Ask the children why the mountain is special. Share pictures of mountain views with the class. What other activities do people enjoy in the mountain snow resorts?

A Cold Winter's Day

On a cold winter's day,
Get a cup of hot cocoa.
Sit by the fire and read a good book.
School's probably canceled
So you can spend time in your private nook.

Send your brother out to shovel the drive.
Get your cuddly teddy bear.
Enjoy your chocolate chip cookies
And be glad your brother's out of your hair!

You can send the family on a ski trip.
You can send them to the store.
But you can stay by the fire
And read tons of books galore!

Ask the children to talk about their favorite winter activity. Is it inside or outside?

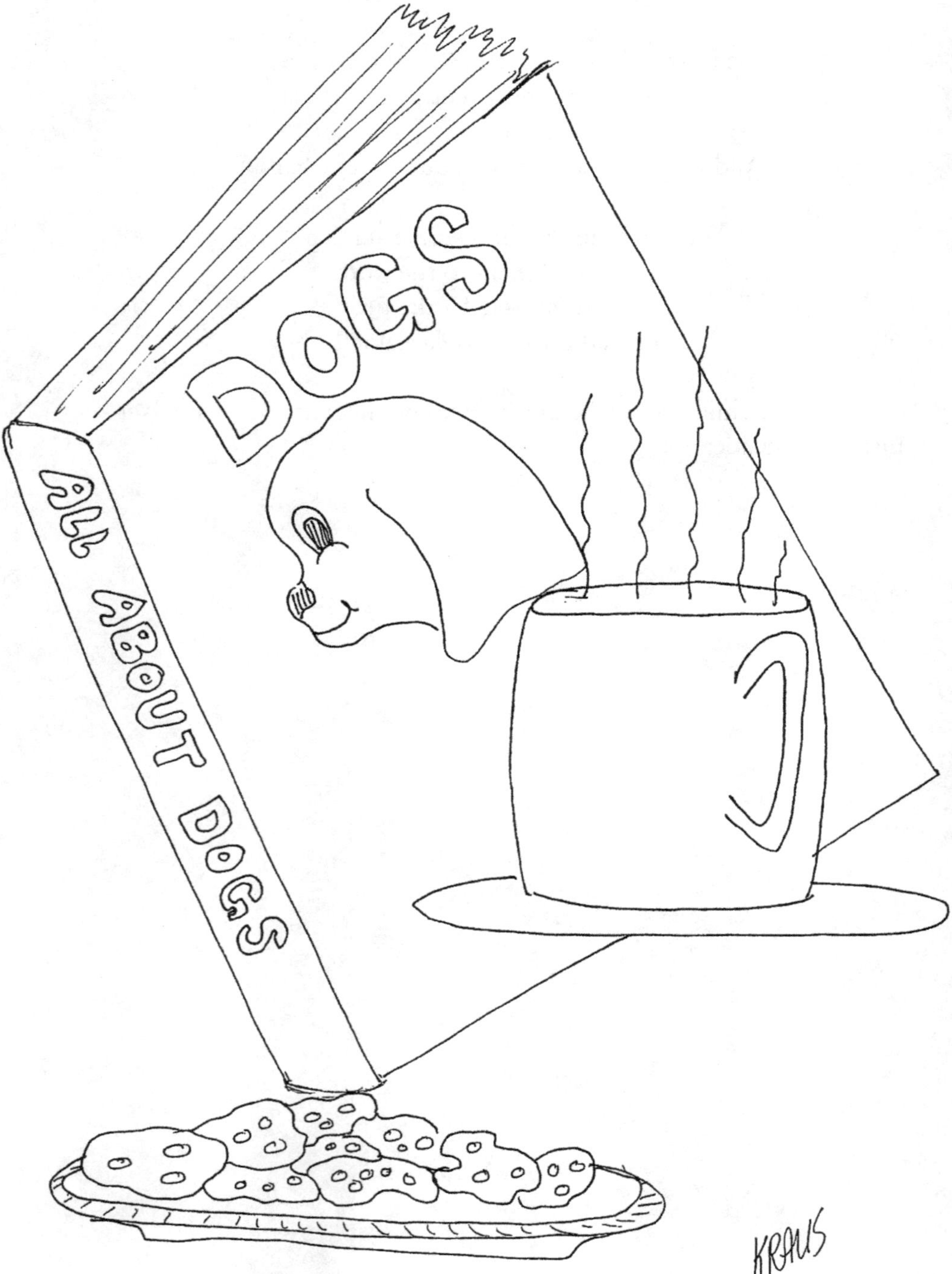
DOGS
ALL ABOUT DOGS
KRAUS

Snowflakes

Snowflakes come in different shapes and sizes.
They can be very big or very small.
They're really awesome crystals
That fascinate us all!

Imagine how many have fallen
Just in one winter's day!
How many are in my snowman
And in the yard where I play!

How hard it is to count so high!
How wondrous they are to see!
They are a gift from the sky above
And they came for you and me.

If you live where there is snow, have the children look at the flakes through a magnifying glass to see the crystals. They can cut their designs from white paper. Hang your "blizzard" to decorate your room.

Snow

Snow is white.
Snow is bright.
Snow is slippery.
What a fright!

Dark Winter Nights

The nights in winter are long and dark.
Short and cold is each passing day.
The sun has traveled far to the south
Where kangaroos jump and play!

Explain the summer and winter solstice to the class. Longitude, latitude, and equator are words to introduce in this discussion. Talk about South America, Australia, and North America. Perhaps all of the continents should be included.

The Happy Snowman

I am a fat and happy man.
I am made of snow.
I have a cap upon my head.
And I like the wind to blow.

The blowing wind is very cold.
It makes me happy here.
I said I like the wind to blow.
It makes me smile with cheer.

Oh no! Oh dear! Here comes the sun!
Now, I can't have my way!
I can't hold my cap in place,
It's far too hot to stay!

Hold on! Here come the clouds and wind.
It's cold enough to stay!
I do enjoy this winter chill.
It's really made my day!

The children will enjoy making an indoor snowman. Buy white trash bags in two different sizes. The small one will be for the head and the larger one will be the body. Stuff both bags with tissue paper or newsprint. Tie the ends. Tie the tied ends together and tape for extra strength. Cut out a red smiling mouth, a nose, and two eyes. Paste the features on the head. A hat can be placed on his head, and a scarf can be wrapped around his neck.

Eskimos

Eskimos live where it's cold. They live in a land of ice.
Each day is like the other. It really isn't nice!
They dress in furs and live in houses made of ice.
If they had any heat at all, the house would melt,
And that isn't very nice!

This presents an opportunity to talk about Eskimos, igloos, and another kind of community. Share pictures of Eskimos doing daily chores for survival. Discuss what people need to survive. Talk about the difference between needs and wants.

Martin Luther King Jr.

One of the great men of history
Lived in the twentieth century.
He marched for freedom and equality.
He fought to preserve our liberty.

We can be proud of our nation's best.
He led his people to pass the test.
And no one would really rest
Until all had found peace and happiness.

We hope his death was not in vain.
Though it caused his family great pain.
Because, in fact, we're all the same.
We're all equal in God's name.

There are many books for children about Martin Luther King Jr. A trip to the library will be helpful. He was a minister, a father, and a leader. He wasn't just for Black people. He was for all the minorities. He wanted people to live together the way the Constitution was written. He wanted equal opportunity for everybody.

Rosa Parks

Rosa Parks created sparks and set the tongues to wagging!
She was brave, her feet to save, when she came home from working!
She rode the bus, started all that fuss, and people did some thinking!

> For freedom true, for the Red, White, and
> Blue, Rosa Parks did what was fitting!

A lot of tension was building in the South during the Civil Rights Movement. A history lesson on slavery, the reason our young nation had slaves, the fact that the Founding Fathers thought it was wrong but couldn't think of a way to abolish it, and many other facts about our country can be taught.

Discuss the indentured servant program and the apprentice system. The colonists needed help developing this new land. England was anxious to have the income from the colonies, but she was not eager to support them, so England began the slavery idea and profited from it. After the Revolution, the slaves stayed. They were in the North as well as the South.

Some plantation owners were very cruel. Others were kind and generous. One slave family was given a large piece of St. Simon's Island in Georgia. Their descendants are still there.

Recommended Reading for the Teacher

Besides *Uncle Tom's Cabin* and *Gone with the Wind,* the teacher should read Eugenia Price's series, *The Savannah Quartet.* Another good book is by Herman Cain, *They Think You're Stupid.* Michael Phillips has written a series, *Shenandoah Sisters,* about two orphans after the Civil War. Many books are written about Tom Jefferson, George Washington, and the Madisons. All of these books will be helpful in understanding the development of slavery, its influence on both White and Black people, and the impact it has today.

Children in the United States are truly mixed together. They're in schools, restaurants, playgrounds, hospitals, and every place people shop and work. There's opportunity everywhere. If children stay away from drugs and the influence of bad adults, they can lead successful lives.

The Colors of Our Country

Our country is a melting pot.
We're all mixed together.
We're yellow, red, black, and white.
We live and work together.

We're Irish, German, Chinese too.
We built this land together.
We worked on railroads; we dug the coal.
We had to work together.

> We're African, English, Indians too.
> We farmed the land together.
> We fought for freedom and equal rights
> But it won't mean much if we're not together!

Discuss the development of our country and the reasons why these nationalities left their homeland to come to the United States. Several ethnic groups are not mentioned in the poem but they are important too. Name them. Discuss the significance of this topic with current events.

In the 1830s, President Jackson ordered the Cherokee tribes to move to Oklahoma. Have the students do a little research on the "Trail of Tears." This is truly an emotional lesson. It can be found on the Internet under "Trail of Tears."

February and Valentine's

February—
Winter month of ice and snow,
Presidents' birthdays, I know,
Valentine's with a special glow,
The shortest month will quickly go.
February—all tied up with a BIG RED BOW!

Valentines

Valentines of red and blue
Are sent to friends, it's true.
"But valentines don't have to be red,
They can be any color," I said.

This poem is to reinforce the color words learned earlier in the year. The children may make valentine shapes of all the colors that need to be reviewed. They may write the color name on the valentine.

Sending Valentines

Valentines of pink and blue
Are sent to friends like me and you,
To tell you that I think you are
Very special!
Yes, you are!

Valentine Cards

Valentines are lots of fun to send to friends, one by one.
Ann likes the ones with lots of lace. You
can't find them just any place.
Bill likes the ones that simply say, "I'm thinking of you today!"
But no matter the card or phrase, it's one of our happiest holidays!

    Valentine's Day became popular in the 1800s. There are quite a few stories about St. Valentine that can be found on the Internet. The month of February is also the supposed time that the birds find their mates. Have the children do a little research and write about their findings.

    It's always fun to make your own valentine cards and decorate them.

Our Presidents

The presidents must be honest.
To their country they must be true.
They must put their country first
In everything they say
And everything they do!

Have the class discuss the following: what it means to "put the country first," the programs the government should support, and what they would do if they were president. How much responsibility should the states have? Counties? Cities? Develop a plan to fund the school system. Include farms, roads, environment, defense, housing, employment, taxes, and transportation in your discussion. Relate the results to the Constitution. What did the Founding Fathers do right? What improvements have been made in the last two hundred years? Discuss the amendments.

My Country

I love my country, the land of the free.
I love its beauty, so pretty to see.
I love it because it's a democracy!

George Washington

He was our first president.
He was honest, brave, and true.
He led his countrymen
When the United States was new.

He lived in a lovely home.
It was Mount Vernon by name.
You can visit it today.
It still looks quite the same.

He was loved by his troops.
He was loved by his wife.
He was adored by his nation.
He was a victor over strife!

George Washington.

Make a Five-Point Star

1. Fold an 8.5 by 10 inch paper in half.

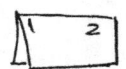

Number the corners 1 and 2.

2. Fold and unfold in half both ways.

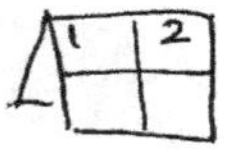

3. Fold corner 1 to meet center line.

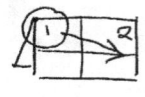

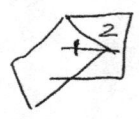

4. Bring corner 1 left till edges meet.

136

5. Bring corner 2 left and fold.

6. Bring corner 2 right till edges meet.

7. Cut at angle.

8. Open up. See your star. You can always start over.

Abraham Lincoln

Lincoln was born in a humble log cabin.
He lived in the middle of a forest.
His father built their little cabin.
Among our presidents, he was the poorest.
He loved books and read a lot.
He taught himself to read and write.
The characters were his only friends.
He read at night by the firelight.

He worked in the fields and chopped the wood.
He grew very tall and strong.
He always did what his parents said.
He had a sense of right and wrong.
He wanted to help his fellow man.
He studied law, upheld the righteous cause.
Believing slavery to be wrong,
He ran for President to change the laws.

The war that followed hurt everyone.
Lots of people lost all they had.
Cities were burned to the ground.
The entire country was sad.
And then John W. Booth shot him in the head.
The man who lived to free each slave
Was laid to rest and remembered best
For the Union he worked to save!

Politics

Politics is what makes the country tick!
We shout and listen to speakers who make us sick!
We vote for our beliefs and hope we win!
We don't want a louse to get in!
We listen carefully to what they say.
We know the winner will rule the day.
He'll decide our laws and taxes too.
He'll control our lives before he's through.
So he'd better be good, he'd better be best,
'Cause if he's bad, there'll be no rest!

Washington and Lincoln Activities

Mount Vernon can be located on a map. Pictures of the house and a map of the plantation grounds can be viewed. The reason the house is close to the river is for the transportation of goods and people. List all the skills a working plantation had to have to take care of all the people living there.

Find reading material about George Washington. Discover what kind of student young George was. What was his favorite activity? Was he someone with whom you would have liked to play? What did he do to prepare himself to lead the Revolution? The class could have a Washington birthday party. Bread pudding is a Southern treat that would be enjoyable. Box mixes can be found at the grocery for bread pudding or everyone could have a slice of cherry pie in honor of Washington's birthday.

The children can make Lincoln's log cabin by rolling brown paper sections into log shapes. Glue the "logs" together to make a log house. Make them the appropriate length to include a door and a window.

Find and read books about young Abe Lincoln. Discover how he felt when his mother died and his father remarried. Would he have been a good friend? Compare his childhood to Washington's. Would you say his home life was dysfunctional? Yet he became a great man because he worked hard and was honest.

What characteristics made these two men great presidents? Compare them to our present president.

The class can write about these two men and illustrate their stories. They may write a small play to entertain another class or friends. The young children may draw a picture. The teacher can help them write a title for their picture.

Perhaps you can find a movie about Abe Lincoln that the class would enjoy. Try the library and the Internet.

SPRINGTIME

March

April

May

March, April, May

These months' lessons cover the changing weather pattern from winter to spring, St. Patrick's Day and leprechauns, Easter, rebirth of nature, Mother's Day, and the joy of being outside in warmer weather. This offers an opportunity to study spring weather patterns, tornados and hurricanes, and to learn how to be safe when these phenomena occur. The children will have fun with the leprechauns and the St. Patrick's Day study. There are several lessons on plants, birds, and forest animals. Directions for making an Easter basket are included. There are Mother's Day projects that can be given to Mother on her special day. This ends the school year.

March

March is windy. March is bright.
It's stormy and it's spring's delight.
Two different seasons are fighting to win
But when it's over, warm weather comes in!

Warmer Weather

March is a little warmer.
The sun's a little brighter.
My heart's a little lighter
Because spring is around the corner!

March Winds

March winds set the hats to flying!
They make you wrap up tight!
They howl and push you all around
And keep you up at night!

But then they make my kite fly high.
They make my soap bubbles scatter.
They can make life a lot of fun
And that's what really matters!

Whatever you wish to do about Easter and Passover is up to you. There is one Easter poem included in this collection.

March, The Month of the Lamb and the Lion

March is the month that stands in the gap.
Winter and Spring argues and scrap.
But there's no controlling the route of the sun,
Warmer weather will soon have begun.

We call Winter the Lion that bellows and blows,
Causing temperatures to drop, bringing the snows,
We call Spring the Lamb that brings a warm breeze,
Encouraging the flowers and the buzzing bees.

Yes, Spring must follow, the seasons ordained
By the Master's hand during His reign,
He put the sun, moon, and stars in the sky
And his power will keep them there till Time draws nigh.

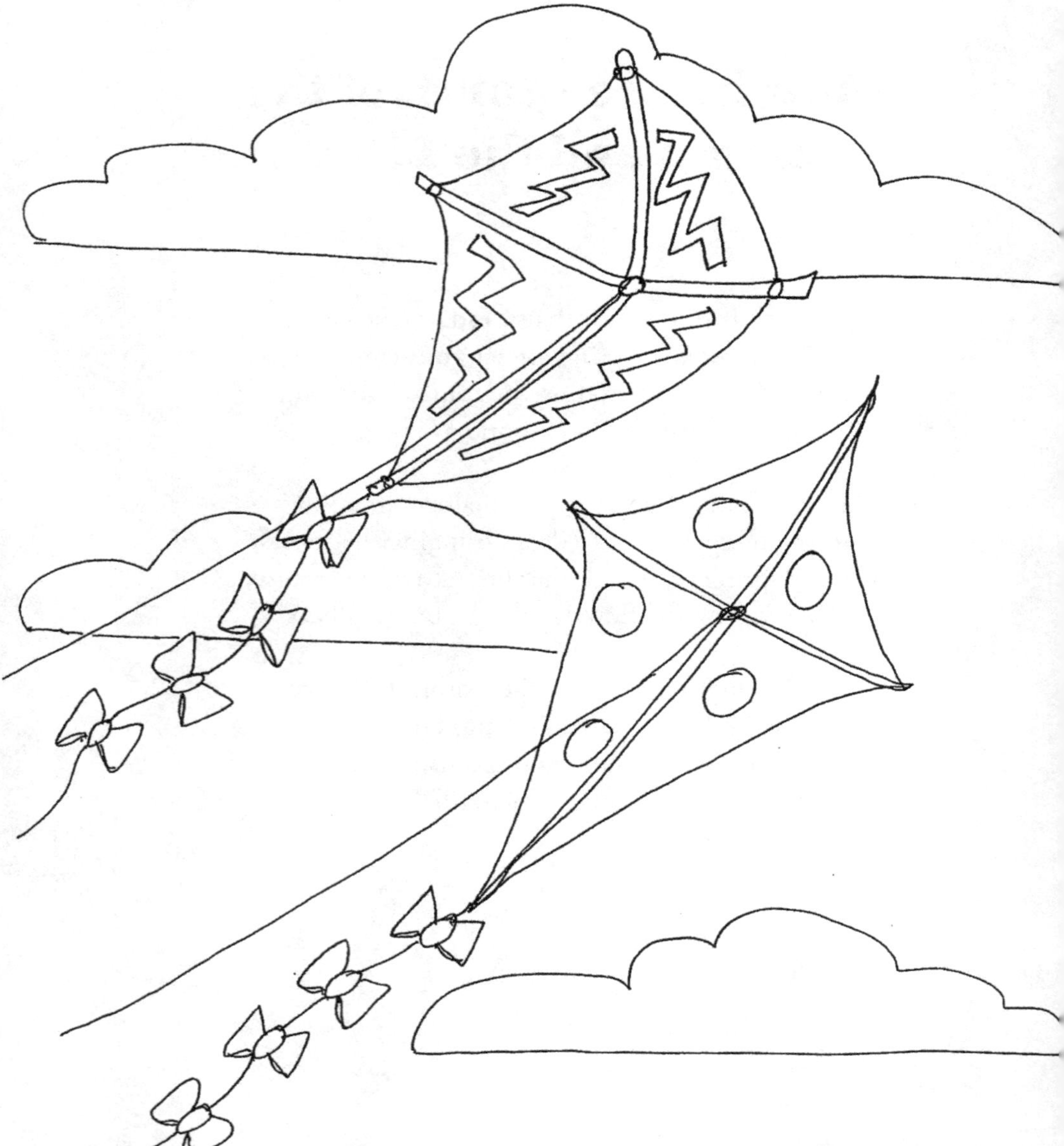
KRAUS

My Kite

See my kite!
It's the one that's red!
It flies so high just over your head!
It's made of paper, two sticks, and some string.
It flies really fast with Zip and Zing!
It's quite a marvelous kite!
I made it all in just one night!

That Nasty Wind

That nasty wind just blew my hat away.
It took my papers and tossed them in the air.
It pushed me all around the yard,
And look what it did to my hair!
That nasty wind is not my friend.
It causes a lot of trouble.
And if that nasty wind keeps blowing,
I mean everything I said and DOUBLE!

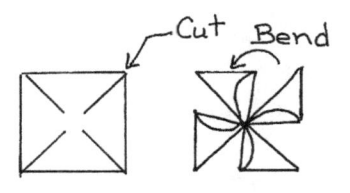

Wind activities

The class can make a pinwheel. Use a square sheet of paper. Fold it twice crosswise. Cut on the fold lines, leaving a space in the middle for stapling the corners. Take a pin and a straw. Pin the pinwheel to the straw. Hold it in the wind or blow on it to make it move.

The class can have a kite day. Each child can bring a kite to fly. Tell them how to hold the string and run with the kites so they won't be disappointed.

Perhaps you can acquire weather balloons and fill them with helium. Have the class prepare notes to put in baggies to tie to the balloons. Include your address. Wait to hear from whomever finds it. Locate the city on the map.

Listen to the weatherman and find the weather map in the paper. Discuss what causes tornados and hurricanes. Where and when are they most likely to occur? What safety precautions should people take for each problem? If you are prepared for a problem, it won't be so scary.

Helium weather balloons may not be allowed. Check with the local authorities.

March Surprises

March is a pleasant month,
Although it has surprises.
It can rain or it can snow.
Maybe the winds will really blow!
But, chances are, the sun will shine.
You should have a super time!

A Walk in Spring

The ice has melted.
The snow is gone.
The polar cold has now moved on.
And as the kids walk,
Just now to the tree,
They can see the wee birds break free.
The babies are born.
They are very small.
They'll snuggle and wait for Mother's call.
Soon they'll be big,
And they'll leap from the nest.
They'll be ready to fly to the east and the west.

Robin

I saw a robin in a tree.
He sang his glad spring song.
He sang, "Cheer up! Cheer up!
Warmer weather will be along!"
Yes, the robin likes to welcome spring.
He's the first sign to appear.
He flies about while it's still cold.
I guess he likes it here.

Spring Flowers

Flowers come in every color.
In every shape and size.
I'll plant some seeds and water them.
They'll bloom before my eyes!

Colorful Flowers

Flowers are all colors.
They're red, yellow, and white.
They come in different sizes.
They're all a different height.
I've seen them blue and orange.
I've seen them purple too.
They grow up from the earth of black.
They streeeetch up...just to see you!

Word study activities

Have the children make a paper kite. Put a string on the kite and attach bowtie papers to the string. Write the words on the bowties. Have them read their kite tail.

The kite could have a sound to study written on the diamond shape. The bowtie tails could be words with that sound. If the sound to be studied is *-ar*, then *-ar* is written on the kite, and *far, star, car,* and *jar* are written on the bowties.

Flowers can be used to review the color words. A garden of designated colors can be designed.

Sounds can be studied on "daisies." The center of the flower has the study sound. The petals have the words. All the flowers can be placed on a bulletin board for spring. The kites can be placed in the sky.

Science

Take a spring walk. Look for signs of spring. Do you see flowers peeking at you? Do you see birds building nests? Keep a list of what you see. Make a *Spring Book* about your observations.

Look for clouds. Draw pictures of the clouds you see. Decide what type of clouds they are and what the names are for each type. What kind of weather does each cloud forecast?

A weather poem to memorize

Red sky at night, sailors' delight! Red sky in the morning, sailors take warning!

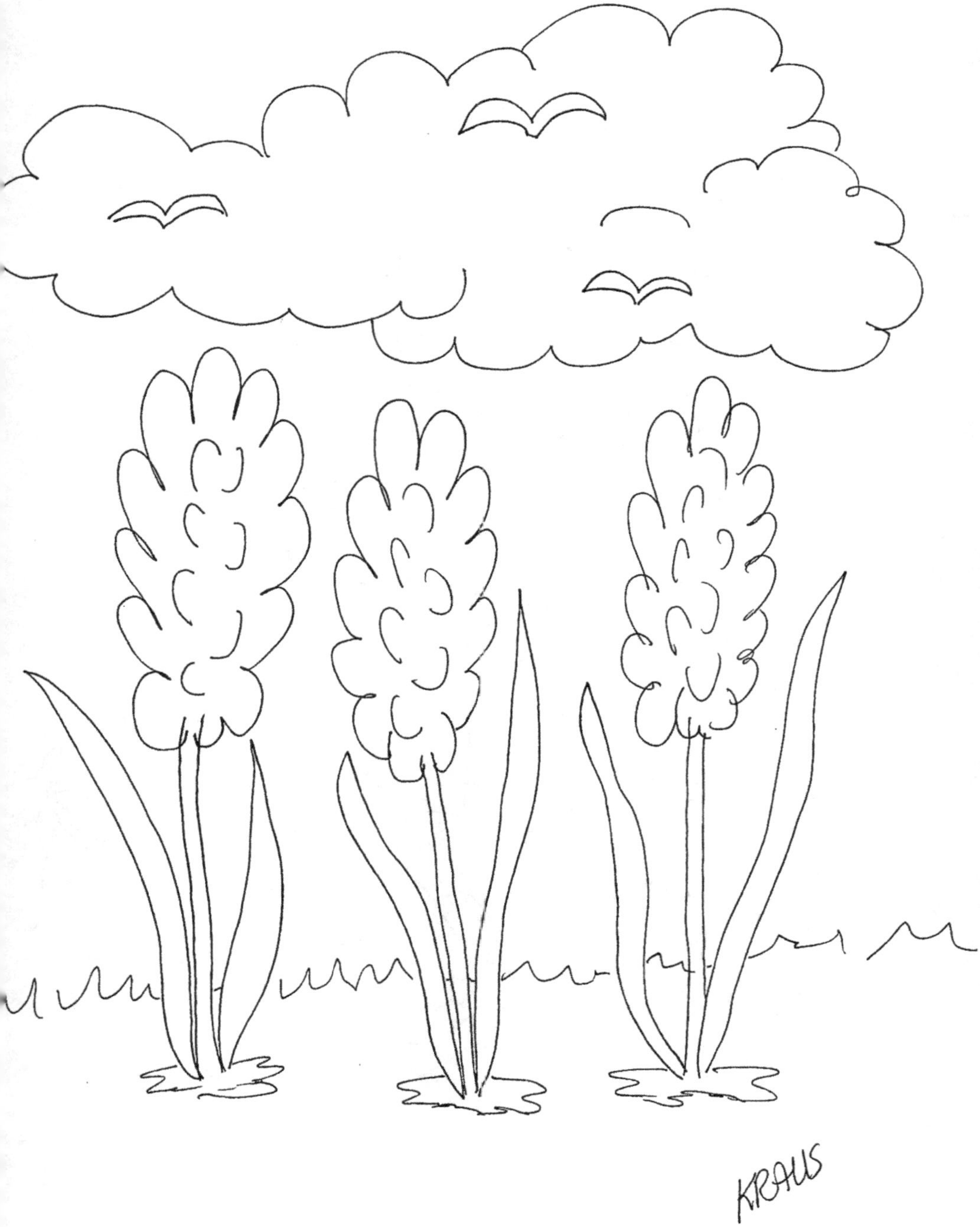
KRAUS

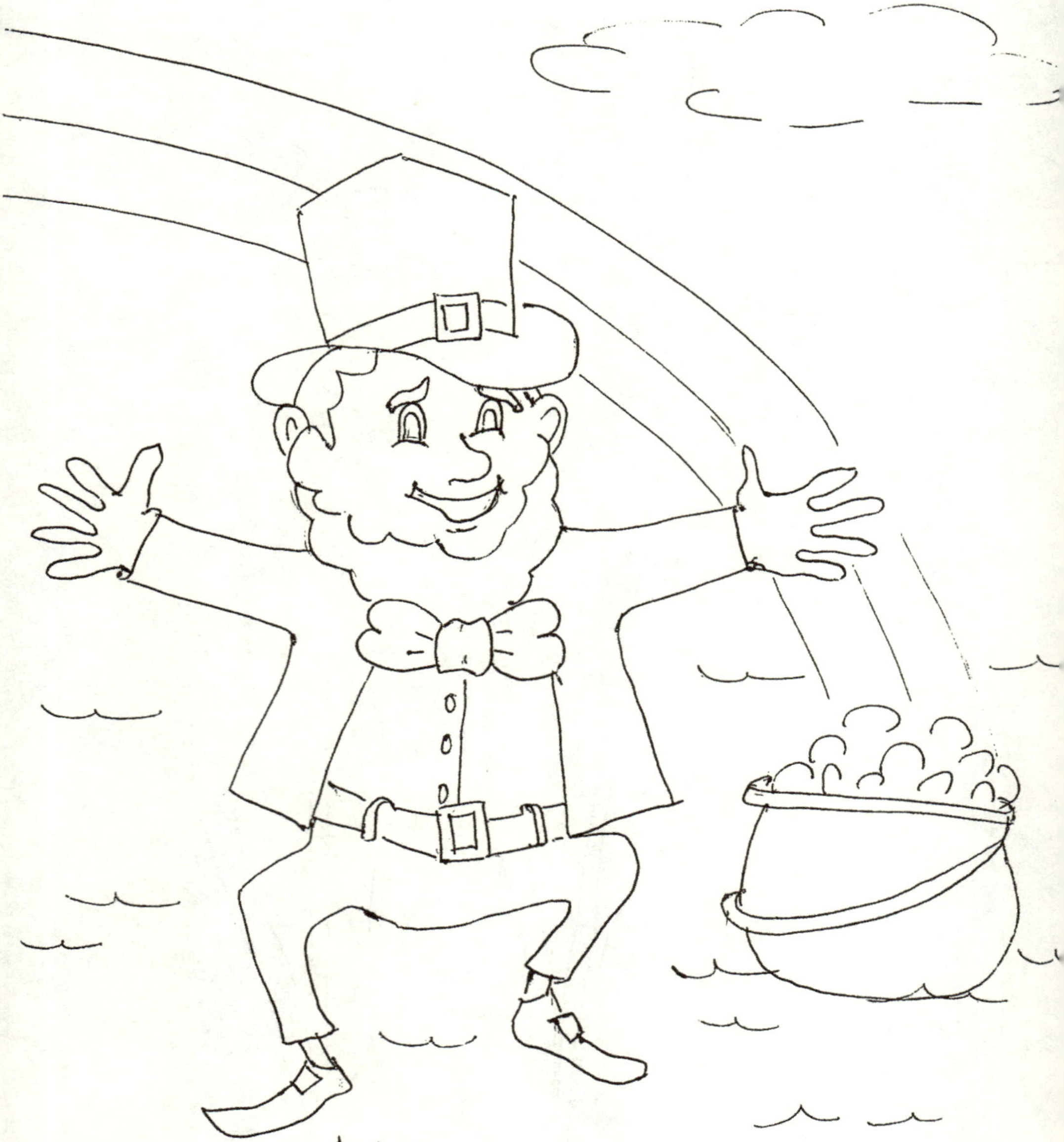

The Little Old Man

The little old man I saw today
Had a twinkle in his eye.
He looked as though he wanted to play
With all the passersby.
He looked so strange, all dressed in green,
Standing there upon the lawn.
Oh mercy and by gosh! Could he have been
A merry leprechaun?

The Leprechaun's Wish

I can see a rainbow this mornin'.
It's pretty in the sky.
I know there's a pot o' gold.
It must be buried here, nearby.
I'm off to find my fortune.
I'm off to find the gold.
I'll clap my hands and dance
When I find my pot o' gold!
I'll buy six big white horses
And I'll parade them on the lawn.
My friends and I'll party…
Oh no! The rainbow is gone!

Creative writing

The children can pretend they actually have a pot of gold. How will they use it? Discuss the possibilities, write them on the board, and have the class use these ideas for a story. Tell them to remember to have a *beginning, middle,* and an *end.* The beginning is the setting, the middle is the problem, and the end is the solution.

Each child could pretend to be a leprechaun and write an autobiography. Include a short study of Ireland and the Blarney Stone.

Each child could write a "Blarney" story.

Saint Patrick's Day

Saint Patrick's Day is a day of fun!
First you put your green clothes on!
Then pack a picnic and grab a chair,
Climb in the car, and you're almost there!

You go into town, looking for the best location
To watch this fantastic celebration.
And there it is, right on the street!
You can sit in front. See all the people you can meet?

Listen now. Listen well. Hear the music begin to swell?
The band is coming. Hear the drum and hear the bell?
Everyone is smiling and wearing green.
It's a very happy scene!

There are a lot people in this parade.
There are lots of floats the kids have made.
There are pets dressed in little green hats,
And there are a few acrobats!

Saint Patrick's Day is a lot of fun.
It's playing all day in the springtime sun!
It's eating lunch in the park and listening to the band.
And being with the family…that's really grand!

Saint Patrick's Day activities

The class can find out who Saint Patrick was, what he did, and why he was important. Find the cities that have really big Saint Patrick's Day parades. New York City and Savannah, Georgia, have big parades. Find these cities on the map.

Make your own parade. The children can make large poster pictures for their float, musical instrument, and pet. They can march around the room, the block, or visit other classrooms.

They may share their research about Saint Patrick with another class. They can write a short play to present or they may want to tell about Ireland. Each child may have something to say. The more children there are in the class, the more facts they can find.

Bartram Bear's Adventures on the First Day of Spring

Bartram had spent the winter in the cave with his mother.
He wanted to be outside to play in the warm weather.
It had been a cold, hard winter in the Smoky Mountains.
He wanted to romp in the green grass and frolic in the fountains.

He knew all the places he wanted to go.
He wanted to see the cabins when they weren't covered with snow.
He could go inside them, explore each nook.
Oh, he would enjoy having a good look.

So Bartram stretched and yawned,
He ambled about and soon he was gone!
He raced over the hills and through the meadows,
He scared all the deer. They ran for the shadows.

He sat down by a stream that was teeming with trout.
He tried to catch one but he missed. His lip made a pout.
But Bartram wasn't unhappy long.
He heard the bees buzzing. He made up a song!

He saw the spring flowers dressed in colors so bright,
He saw violets and daisies. He loved everything in sight.
He picked quite a few for his mother that day.
He was really proud of his lovely bouquet.

He looked at the hills glowing in the morning sun.
He had a grand feeling of wanting to run.
The dogwood trees were all in bloom.
He was happy to have so much running room.

And then his face changed from joy to fear!
The clouds were gathering. A storm was coming here!
He was miles from his cave and from his mother.
He had to find some place quickly for cover.

Then he remembered the pioneer cabins.
They were in the park where the road bends.
It was the old road that the tourists like.
They can drive their car or go for a hike.

So he ran for the shelter of the cabins near the town.
He got there just before the rain came thundering down.
He had managed to save his mother's bouquet.
It made him happy to know the flowers were okay.

The cabin was the perfect place to stay.
It was warm and dry, and he liked it that way.
But it wasn't long before he heard running.
He looked up in time to see two people coming!

What would he do if they picked his house?
He was scared, so scared he trembled like a mouse.
Yet, he thought, *I could give them fits*!
Maybe I could scare them out of their wits!

He was getting ready to make his most fierce noise
When, through the door, came two loud little boys.
They were frightened by the pouring rain,
And they shouted and squealed as if in pain.

Bartram huddled in one corner in the dark.
He studied the two boys who were visiting the park.
He decided they looked harmless enough.
And he concluded that they weren't very tough.

One of them was crying. He was extremely upset.
The older one was his brother, Bartram would bet.
The young one just kept sobbing, so full of fright.
Bartram stayed in the corner, hiding out of sight.

The older boy saw a few flowers on the floor.
He knew that someone else must be there,
perhaps behind the door…
He looked there…and then he looked carefully in each dark place…
His eyes grew big when he saw the bear's furry face!

Well, Bartram didn't know what to do.
He was just a little baby too.
The older boy retreated to where his brother was crying.
Bartram followed him softly, whining and sighing.

The kids were scared of Bartram, but they tried to look brave.
And Bartram was wishing he was home in his cave.
They sat there together in the middle of the room.
And as they huddled for warmth, the thunder went BOOM!

Meanwhile, Bartram's mother was full of despair.
Where oh where was her baby bear?
She started out in the terrible rain,
Thinking she would never see him again.

She looked in the meadow, straining to see.
She went by the stream where the rapids ran free.
Danger seemed to lurk just everywhere.
She was certain that trouble had found Bartram Bear!

And the boys' mom and dad were upset too.
They had no idea where to look, what to do!
They had gone to Gatlinburg on a holiday.
And now this disaster had come their way.

They had been camping near the National Park.
They had come in the spring, had come for a lark.
The boys had gone hiking about an hour ago,
Before the storm came with its gusto and blow.

They thought of the places the boys could be.
Would they be in the cabins? They had to see.
So the boys' parents went up the back path,
While Mama Bear came down, concealing her wrath.

She would certainly scold her dear Bartram Bear.
She disapproved of his giving her such a scare.
Who would reach the cabin first?
If Mama Bear did, the boys could be hurt…or worse.

But, fortunately, the parents arrived with just minutes to spare.
They grabbed their boys and scurried away from there.
Bartram sat bewildered on the floor.
When he looked up, he saw Mama at the door.

Mama was about to give Bartram a thrashing,
But what's this? Bartram was smiling.
He was so glad to see her; she forgot she was mad.
And the two of them were soon happy and glad.

Bartram proudly gave her the precious bouquet.
The sun came out to finish the day.
Bartram and his mama were snug in their cave.
And while Bartram slept, he dreamed of King Bartram, the Brave!

Bartram Bear Activities

Social studies

1. Locate the Smoky Mountains on the map. Find the city of Gatlinburg, Tennessee. Ask the children if they have visited a state park/national park. Locate these on the map and label them, if it's possible.
2. Discover why we have national parks/state parks and which president began to set aside land for these parks.
3. Make a list of the parks the class has visited. Make a time line that shows the years those parks were established. Discuss the history of each area. Perhaps the children can bring pictures from their trips to share.
4. Pretend the class is a pioneer group moving into the Smoky Mountains. Make a list of what you need to live. Make a map of your farm and other houses and farms. Show what crops and animals you have.
5. Include a study of preparing for the different seasons.
6. John Bartram was an early scientist in America. He studied plants and drew their pictures. Do a little research to find out more about him. Why was his work important?
7. Take a class walk. Pretend you are a scientist making a plant study. Draw your pictures. Label your plant. Tell where you found it. How tall was it? What color was it? Did it have a flower? How can it be used? Honey? Medicine? Dye? Food? Decoration? This overlaps social studies and science.

Science

1. Discuss hibernation. Talk about other animals that hibernate.
2. March 22nd is the first day of spring. Explain why we know when spring begins. Use the globe and a yellow tennis ball to help the children visualize the equinox.
3. Use a reference book or the Internet to find the spring wildflowers that Bartram saw as he walked through the park. Make a display of the variety of flowers.
4. Find and show pictures of mountain streams. Are these streams dangerous in the spring and why?
5. Insects are helpful to the plants and to the fish. Why are they helpful? What kinds of insects do you know live in the Smoky Mountains?

Art

1. Make three-dimensional flowers that could be found in the mountains. Use curly paper strips and frayed circles to make the flowers. Label the pictures.
2. Draw pictures to illustrate Bartram's adventures. Give the pictures a title. Arrange them in the proper sequence.
3. Look carefully at each picture. Count the details in each picture.
4. Make furry bears with curly brown paper strips. Use the bears on a bulletin board of the Smoky Mountain National Park. Make rolled log cabins in your park picture. Use pink and white paper squares glued to tree trunks to make dogwood trees. Perhaps you could make a few wild animals too.
5. Design a trout. Label the trout. List the details about this fish. Length, weight, color, taste, what it eats, and where to find it. Use facts or be creative.

Language arts

1. Read the story to the class. Discuss any new words.
2. Ask the class several comprehension questions. Have them find and read their answers.
3. Take turns reading the verses. It's all right to take a few days to do this story.

Several questions

1. Why was Bartram in the cave all winter?
2. Where did he want to go and why?
3. What animals in the story did he see?
4. What does the word *teeming* mean?
5. Why did he *pout?*
6. What flowers did he see? Trees? Name other plants he would have seen.
7. When did his attitude about spring change?
8. Where did he go for shelter?
9. Why was the family visiting the park? Name as many reasons as you can.
10. Why weren't the children and the bear afraid of each other?
11. What could have happened if Mama Bear arrived first?
12. Is it a good idea to wander far away from your parents? Why not?
13. Who wandered?
14. What part of the story could really happen?
15. What part is make-believe?
16. Why did Bartram Bear dream about being King Bartram?

April

April Showers Bring May Flowers

"April showers bring May flowers,"
So the saying goes.
So be alert and watch the dirt
For tulips standing in their rows.

"April showers bring May flowers,"
So the saying goes,
So look around and watch the ground,
You might see a lovely rose.

Lots of flowers, fed by showers,
Up from the ground they rise.
Stems of green are often seen.
They bloom before my eyes.

The Rain

The rain is a marvelous, fantastic thing.
It makes people happy enough to sing.
We're glad to have rain to water the plants,
And the rain on the roof sounds like elves at a dance.
The puddles are great for my splashing feet,
But it sure is hard to have to stay neat!

Working in the Garden

We went to the store to buy our flowers.
We saw red ones, yellow ones, and blue ones too.
It was hard to decide what we wanted to do.
We must have spent an hour or two.
The ones we bought were fresh and bold, not a bit of brown.
They would make our garden the best in town.
Each one in the family picked out a plant.
Then home we went with high hopes for spring.
We waited for our flowers to do their thing.
They were supposed to get bigger.
They were to bloom big and bright.
But what a surprise we had overnight!
Our flowers had grown out-of-sight!
We had all bought sunflowers!

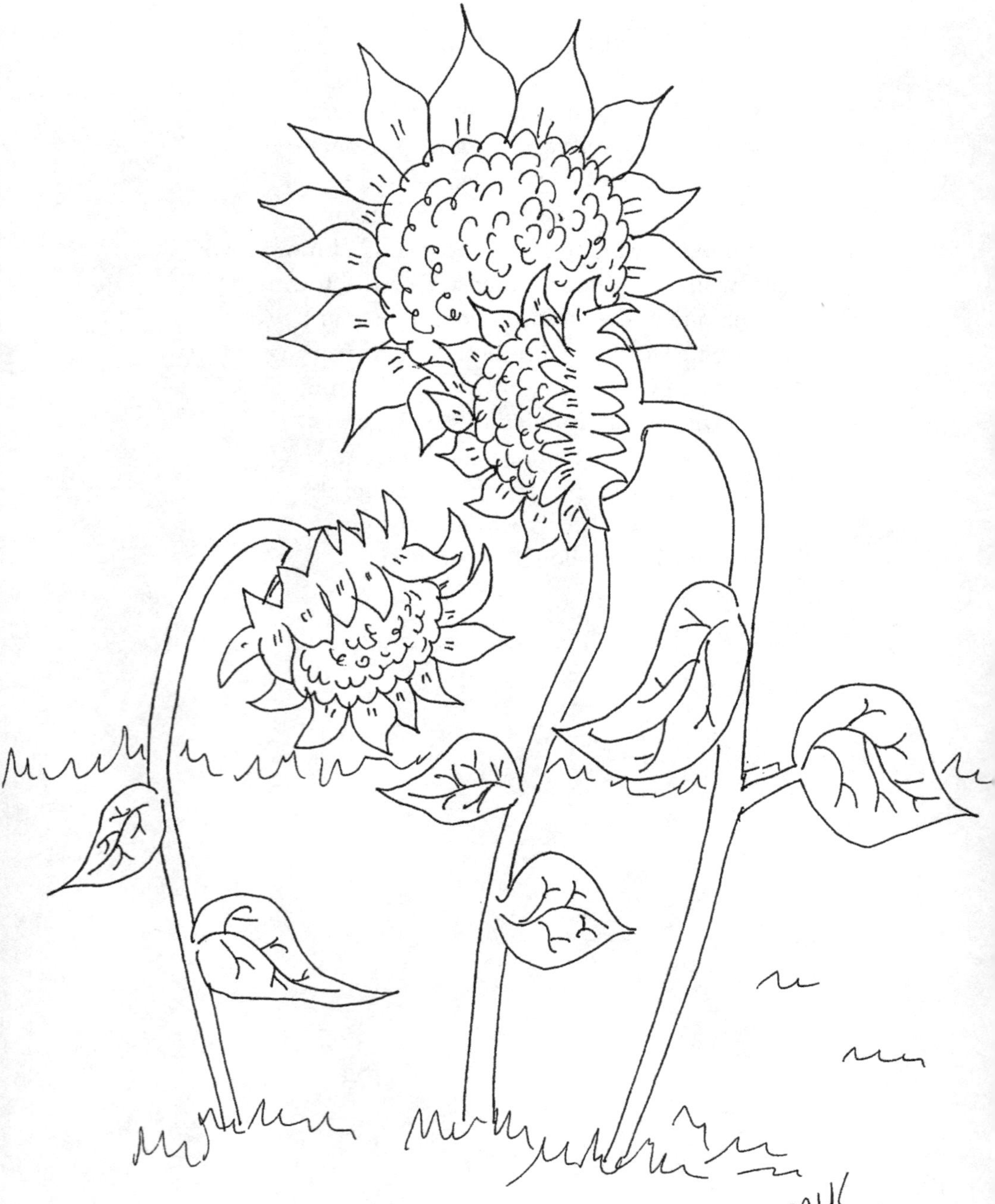
KRAUS

Follow the Raindrop

Once upon a time in a sky far away
Lived a happy cloud all puffy and gray.
Water made the cloud look that way.
And it was growing bigger day by day.

It wasn't very long 'til the cloud was round.
The raindrops would fall upon the ground.
The falling raindrops made a plunkety sound,
And drizzled and frizzled all over the town.

But how did that cloud fill with water that way?
Why did the raindrops gather in a sky far away?
Out at sea the sun heated them one day,
Evaporated raindrops floated up, up this way.

Then the cloud was pushed by the wind over the land
Until it became very large and quite grand.
It grew and grew and shadowed the land.
Raindrops fell on the farms…and on my hand!

Well, now the ground is soaking wet.
Puddles are everywhere, you can bet!
But the sun will come out—it hasn't just yet—
And dry up the puddles, no need to fret.

Then the raindrops will ascend to the sky.
They'll gather into clouds by and by.

And it won't be long 'til they're heavy...my oh my!
Then it will rain again. Try to stay dry!

Activities for rain

1. Describe different types of rain: sprinkling, downpour, thunderstorm, and blowing rain.
2. Talk about the different types of clouds: ones that mean a good day and ones that mean bad weather is coming.
3. Take a walk outside to observe the clouds. Decide what kind of day it is or will be by looking at the clouds.
4. Make raindrops for the bulletin board. Make a big puffy cloud in the sky. Put the ocean nearby and a shiny sun above the big dark cloud.
5. The children can write a short poem for their raindrop.

> *Little Raindrop in the sky,*
> *Little Raindrop ready to cry,*
> *Little Raindrop let me say,*
> *Rain on someone else today!*

6. Do a word family study for *sky* and *day*. The children can make their list on big raindrops or clouds.
7. Fill a jar with water. Mark the level with a marker. Watch the water evaporate by marking each week on the jar (or day, depending on the size of the jar).
8. Discuss how people dress when it rains. Make pictures of umbrellas and boots.
9. Word family study words could be written on a big boot and on a big umbrella.
10. Read stories to the children about rainy day experiences.
11. Use the rain poem to start a study of the *r* sound. List other words that start with *r*.

12. Perhaps you could study *st-*, *cl-*, *u-*, *b-*, *s-*, *sk-/sc-* sounds too. Look for these sounds at the beginning and the ends of words. Make a list of the words that the children find.
13. The children can do an *ou-* study by writing words with that sound on a cloud. *Out* is acceptable, but *soup* is not. Explain to the children that the sound being studied is *ou-* as in *cloud*.

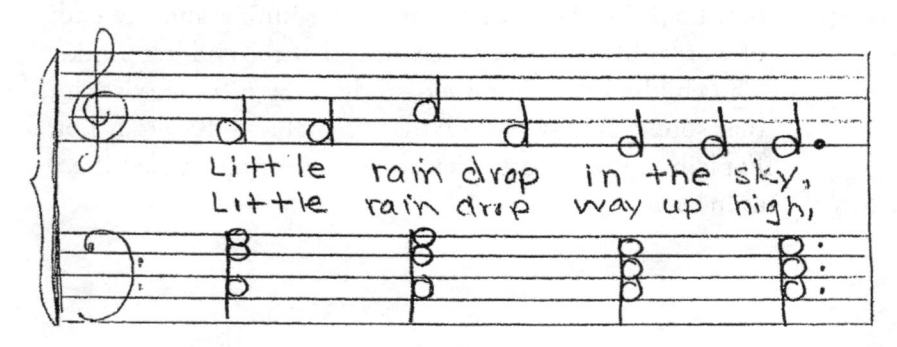

Little Raindrop.

Little rain drop in the sky,
Little rain drop way up high,

Little rain drop ready to cry,
Little rain drop, please don't cry.

Little rain drop let me say
Little rain drop, be on your way.

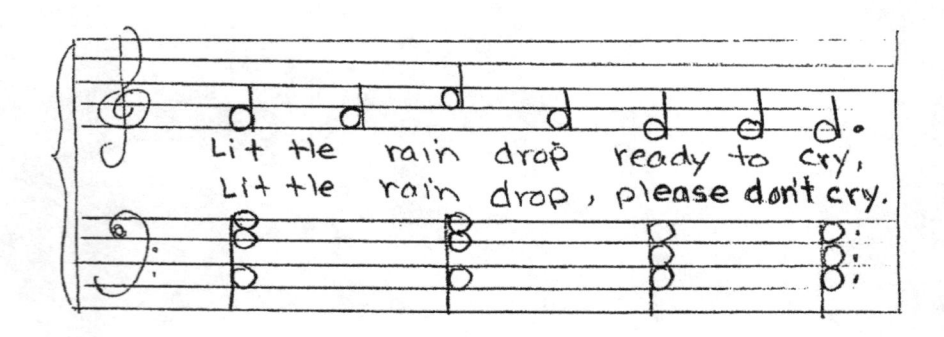

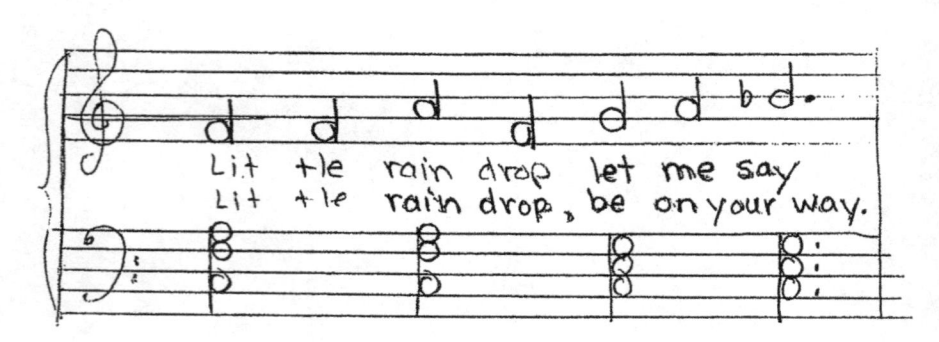

KRAUS

Rain on some one else to day.
Rain on some one else to day.

KRAUS

Easter

Easter is a special time.
For family and friends, it's the best.
We color hardboiled eggs
And dress in our Sunday best!
Sometimes it snows or it could rain.
We don't really mind the weather.
What's nice to know is that God cares
And that we're all together!

Julie's Special Yellow Tulips

Those enchanting tulips that beckon with glee caused
the biggest amount of trouble you ever did see!

Big yellow tulips inviting in the spring,
Big yellow tulips caused my heart to sing,
Big yellow tulips dancing with the breeze,
Big yellow tulips beckoning with ease.

Those big yellow tulips said, "Come over here!"
So I tiptoed carefully without any fear,
Kneeled on my skinned-up knees,
And plucked the biggest bouquet you ever did see!

I was so proud of my brilliant success
That I didn't see I had left the garden in a mess!

I thought Mother would be as thrilled as I…
But all she did was stare…and cry!

Those yellow tulips, so lovely to see,
Had surely brought bad luck to me!
My mother was really quite upset!
And I still remember it all—I can't forget.

So when you see a garden in full bloom,
Remember those tulips that sealed my doom.
Then leave them growing right where they are.
Don't touch! You'll be better off, by far!

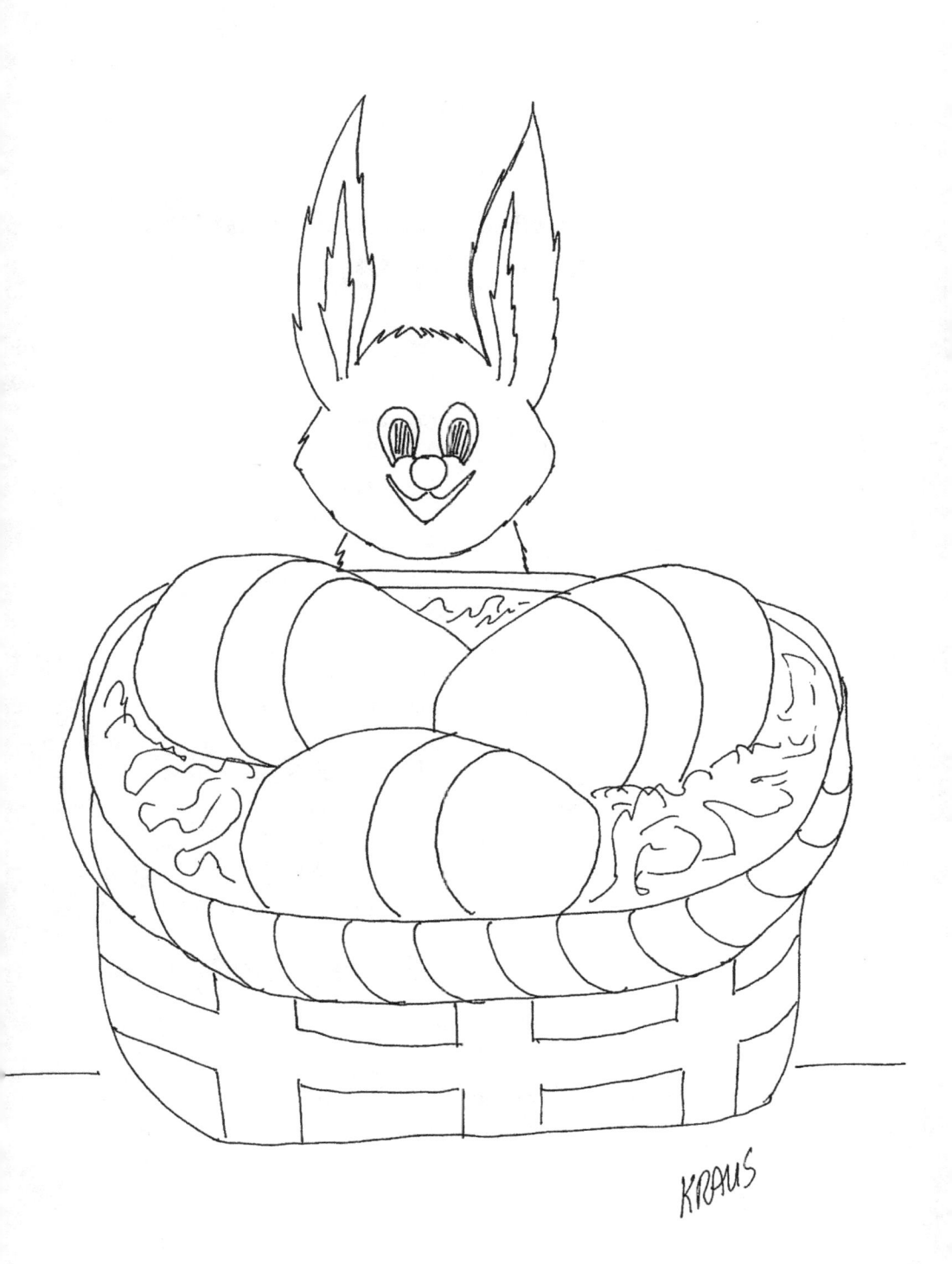
KRAUS

Easter Basket and Mother's Day Gift Ideas

For the Easter basket, the children may weave a strip of colored paper through a green grape tomato basket from the grocery. Fill the basket with shredded colored paper. Put their Easter Bunny gift in it.

There are little tomato baskets that are all clear plastic with a hinge lid. Have the children weave their paper strips and glue them on the plastic. They will need to be patient while the glue dries. They also need to measure carefully so the woven paper sheet fits the basket.

Another suggestion is to fold a large sheet of paper into sixteen parts. Cut on the outside folds and shape the paper into a basket.

Of course, there's the old shoebox basket. The children may glue their woven paper sheets on the box. This will be easier than gluing paper on the plastic.

Easter Bunnies can be made with cotton balls. Draw a bunny. Cover the bunny with cotton balls. Give him pink paper ears. He can have big paper eyes. Cut out paper eggs to glue on the picture.

Sheep can be made the same way.

The bunnies and sheep may be glued on to the children's baskets.

Paper basket

Fold paper into sixteen parts. Dotted lines are the fold lines. Cut on the solid line. Glue ends A and B together on the inside of C.

Glue D and E together on the inside of F. Fold the extra top of C and F over A and B and D and E.

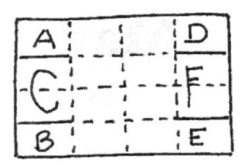

Cotton bunny and sheep

Draw the bunny. Cover him with cotton balls. Put a thin pink paper strip over his ears for the inside of his ears. Do the same with the sheep. Put a pink nose on the bunny and a black nose on the sheep.

For Mother's Day, the children can decorate a cleaned soup can by painting it or gluing a collage on it. They may decide to just simply wrap it in tinfoil. After the can is ready, put potting soil in the can. Be sure to put some pebbles in the bottom so the water is able drain away from the roots of the plant. The children may buy a plant or grow one. If you decide to grow one, start early enough to have a nice plant by Mother's Day.

Make a card for Mother. Tell her three or four things you will do for her around the house.

Use cornstarch clay to make a ring holder. The directions are on the box.

May

A Day in May

A day in May is pleasant.
It's warm and carefree bright.
We've just finished up with winter
And we know everything is all right!

Baby Yellow Chicks

Little baby chicks are as cute as they can be.
They're yellow and fluffy and sweet.
You can see them bobbing and hopping about
On their teeny tiny red feet.

Mother's Day

For my very special mother
On Mother's Day.
"You're the very best mother,"
Is what I want to say.
I love you all the time,
Each and every day.
You're just the very best
In every single way!

Birthdays

Birthdays are such wonderful events.
We celebrate with friends.
We eat cake and ice cream
And hope it never ends!

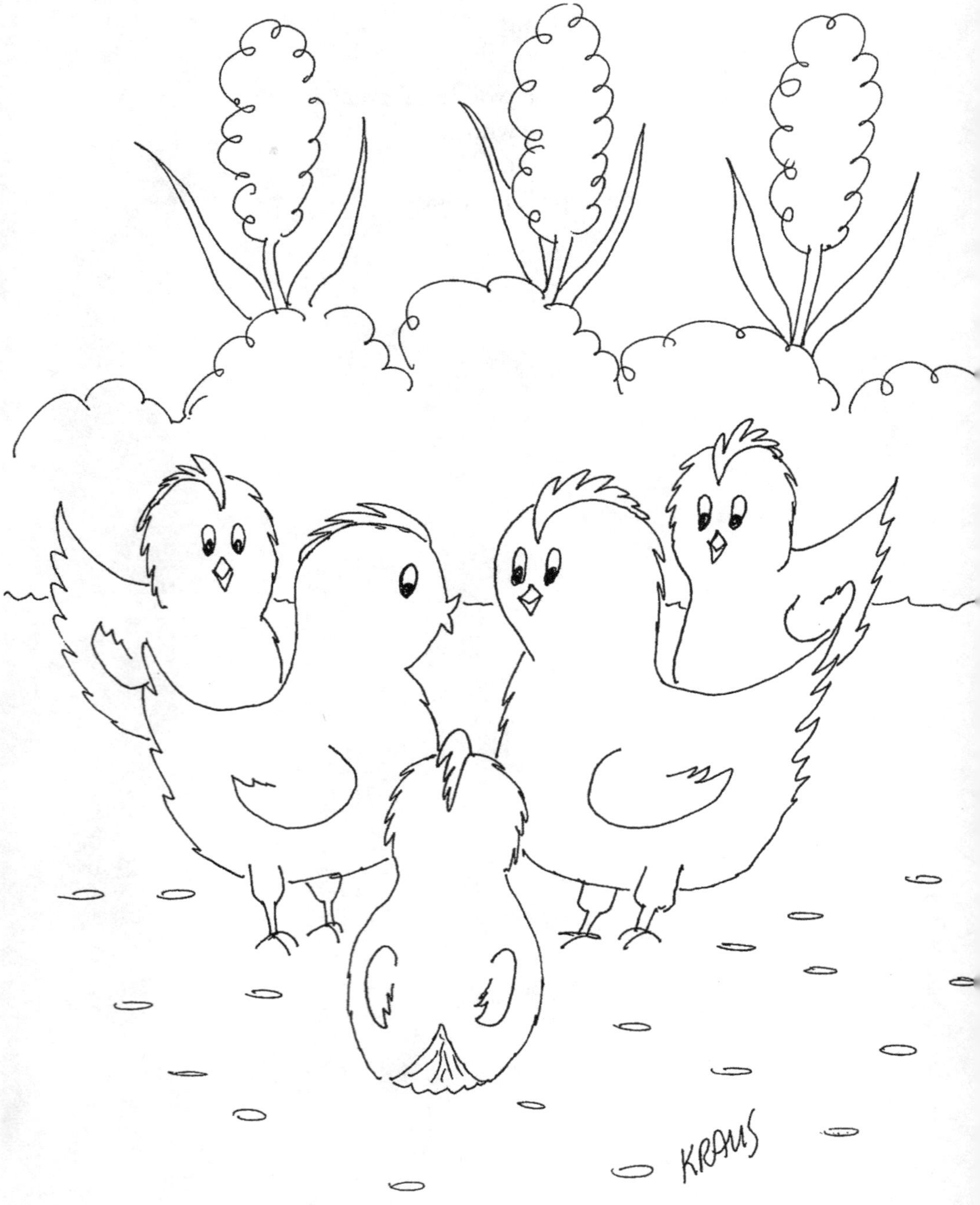
KRAUS

KRAUS

SUMMER

June and July
Vacation Time

June

Oh, June, time of golden sun,
When pools open
And the children leave their books
To dash across the fields on the run.
That old schoolwork is all done and time for fishin' has begun!

The Day School Is Out

On the day that school is out
I get so all excited!
I just want to skip and shout
And think about the things I'd like to do.
I could go swimmin' every day,
I could play baseball too.
They're a lot of games to play,
With all my friends, old and new!
I looked forward to this day all year.
I wanted it more than life, you know!
But now that it's really here,
I miss my teachers so.

Summer Vacation

Summer is a wonderful season.
It's time to relax, go barefoot, and play ball.
It's time to go swimming, visit Grandma,
Sleep late in the morning...

I can have it all!
No one cares if I did my homework.
No one even asks me if I read a book.
But you know what's really funny
Is that I miss my friends, my teachers,
And my books.

Summer

June to July and August

- The summer months are unstructured and full of adventure. The following poems are about animals that the children will see in the woods, at the beach, by the pond, and on the farm. Wherever they go during the summer, they should practice their skills. This practice should be fun. Remember, it's their vacation.
- The children may keep a journal to record their summer activities. Be sure they write at least one sentence about the day. Have them draw a picture to illustrate that activity.
- Review the initial sounds by playing the "sound" game in the car. Make a predetermined list of sounds to find. Use billboards and license plates to find these sounds. Everyone should play. Record the word and/or letter next to the list. Perhaps a bingo type card could be given to each passenger. Have a prize for the winner. Maybe they can choose the restaurant or win a dessert at dinner.
- Look out the window. See a scene that is the setting for a fairy tale. Write a story about what could happen. Have a hero in the story that has a number of problems to solve.
- Review the color words by looking for a *white* horse, a *red* house, a *yellow* flower, etc. The words could be written on

a card so the children would have to read them to score a point. Check them off the list as the words are found.
- Keep a list of vowel sound families. The word for the day may be *knee*. List the words they see with an *ee-* sound. Include the other spellings for the sound.
- If you visit a historical place, purchase books appropriate for your child at the visitor's center. Besides learning about the history, important reading skills can be reviewed as a fun activity. Coloring books have good story starter pictures. Have paper ready for a good story.
- When you go to the grocery, have the child read the list to you to help you shop. If they want something special, have your child write his list for you.
- When you go to the restaurant, have that prepared bingo card ready with menu words written on it. The child can color the words he finds. He gets points for a *T*, and *X*, and/ or an *I*, besides the usual straight line across. The points can be used for earning pennies or nickels.
- A few word games can be played in the house. Have word cards ready with the words you want to review. Put five cards on the table face up. Put a small button under one card. The child is to find the button, but he must read the card before he can look under the card. The adult or other children take turns reading the cards until the button is found. The one who finds the button may hide the button for the next round.
- Have the child make labels for the nouns that are in the house. He can write his words on Post-its. Remove the labels in the evening so he can replace them the following day. Make a game of it.
- Use the magnetic letters to spell words on the refrigerator.
- Always display his work. Develop pride in doing the best work possible. It may not be best by your standards, but it should be the best the child can do.

- Try to stop a game right before it reaches its zenith of enjoyment. This will make the child want to do it again. He will be bored if the game goes too long and frustrated if the game is too hard.
- Have an ongoing adjective list. Try to make the world's longest list of adjectives. Do the same with synonyms and antonyms if the child wants to do it.
- Write antonym slogans. "Summer's cool because summer's hot"; "Don't make a big deal out of small stuff."
- Make a face on a paper plate. Cut a hole for the mouth. Put a second smaller plate behind the "face" plate that has words written on it that will appear through the mouth. Secure it with a brad. Turn the smaller plate so that each word may be read through the mouth window. These words can be a list or they can have a message such as "Bill is a very good boy!" or "Would you like to go to the ice cream store?"
- Have a weekly cooking day. Designate activities if you are involving more than one child. One can read, one can measure, one can stir, and one can pour/spoon into a pan or put on the cookie sheet.
- Make a summer piñata. Use wire to make the frame. Cover the frame with newspaper strips that have been dipped in liquid starch. Let dry. When the piñata is dry, the children may paint it. Name the piñata and write a "biography" for it.

Summer Poems

Father's Day

Happy Father's Day to you, Dad.
When it comes to being the best,
　I know right where to look.
No one will ever take your place.
　You're the greatest in my book!

For Dad

Daddy, I think you're swell.
You're always there for me.
So these HUGS are yours.
They come especially from me!

If You Should See a Frog

Mr. Fancy Frog

This little frog is happy today.
He's going to a Frog Hop right away.
He's dressed up and ready to go.
He's wearing a tie tied up in a bow.

He'll wave his hands and slide his feet.
He'll hop around to the music's beat.
He'll hold his girl and dance about.
He'll give her a swing and she'll shout!

They'll tap their feet, march hand in hand.
Oh they'll really enjoy this band...
Oh my! His foot is caught in the door!
He won't be able to dance anymore.

Poor Mr. Frog sits all alone.
His foot hurts all the way to the bone.
But Miss Froggie comes to his aid.
She nurses his foot so he's not afraid.

Soon he's feeling quite a lot better.
He helps Miss Froggie with her dressy sweater.
Now they're off to have a ball.
He won't have to miss the dance after all.

They hop and they dance with zip and zeal.
My! Mr. Frog has great frog appeal!
Miss Froggie is swept right off her feet.
And Mr. Frog thinks, *Miss Froggie is very sweet*!

He soon asks her to marry him.
She says, "Yes, but I want it proper and prim."
Now the rest of their lives will be happy and bright
All because of a dance on Friday night.

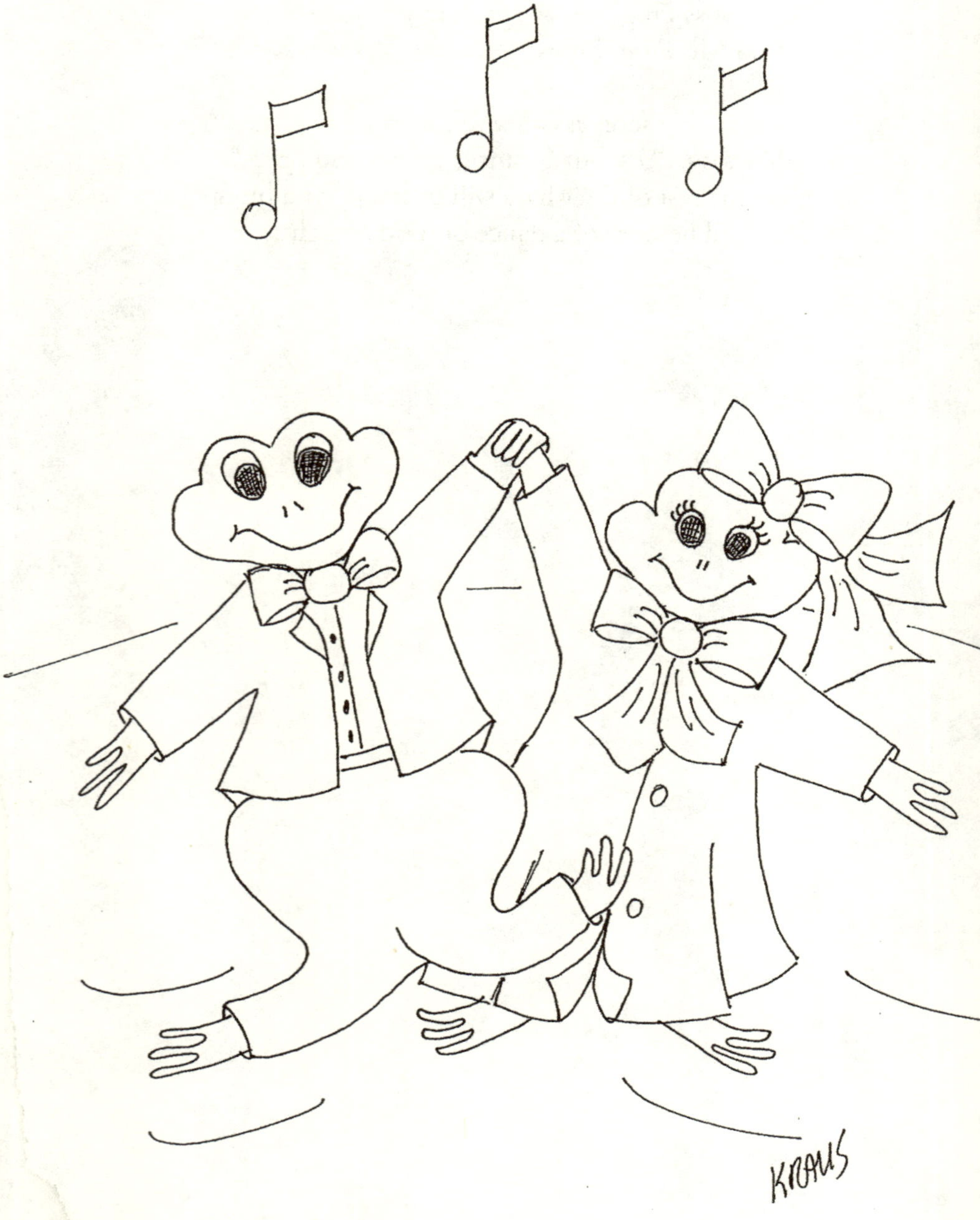
KRAUS

A Walk in the Woods

The Little Woodland Animals

Many little creatures live in the woods nearby.
Lots of squirrels, in a hurry, scurry all around.
See them race across the grass and scamper up a tree.
Their feet don't touch the ground!

They're not like the rabbit that seems so deep in thought.
He nibbles on his blade of grass, then he sniffs the air.
He's sure of where he's going and he knows why
He's hopping there!

The birds tend to raise a ruckus and a fuss.
"Don't bother me!" and "Go away!" they loudly exclaim.
They're not very friendly as they clamor through the sky.
Being nice is not their game!

Foxes might live here too. But they're never seen.
They're very, very clever and know how to sneak.
They raise their pups in secret dens, tucked away
From where others peek!

The woods are full of creatures that make their home right here.
For them, it must be quite an awesome spot.
But I prefer my comfy house 'cause I have cold air when it's HOT!

Several ideas for discussion:

1. How did air-conditioning influence our economy? Growth in the South and the Southwest? Employment? Auto travel?
2. Can you think of other inventions that have helped people? Name them.
3. Perhaps you can study about the people who invented them.
4. What's your favorite invention and why?
5. What would you like to invent and why?
6. What animals live near you? What are their personalities?

203

On the Beach

The Mermaid Princess

Come! Look who came over to play.
It's a mermaid princess out for the day.
She's riding a seahorse, big and bold.
She's wearing pearls and a crown of gold.
She lives on the mountain in the sea,
In a castle that's as big as can be.
It's a castle made of sparkling sand
And it's better than any found on land.
The water there is a lovely blue.
All who see it know that this is true.
So when you're swimming near the beach,
Look! See if a mermaid is within your reach.

The Fish Who Liked to Play

I'm a fish in the water. I'm a fish in the sea.
I'm a fish looking for friends who will come play with me.
Then one fish came over. Soon two fish came to play.
Three of us swam in the water. We played in the water all day.

Starfish

The starfish live in the water.
The starfish live in the sea.
They sleep on the sand of the ocean.
They are as happy as can be.
Who wants to play with the starfish?
Who wants to find them on the shore?
Katie and Ellie like the starfish.
They come each day to find more.
They come early in the morning.
They come to stay all day.
They come to find all the starfish.
They come to see them play.

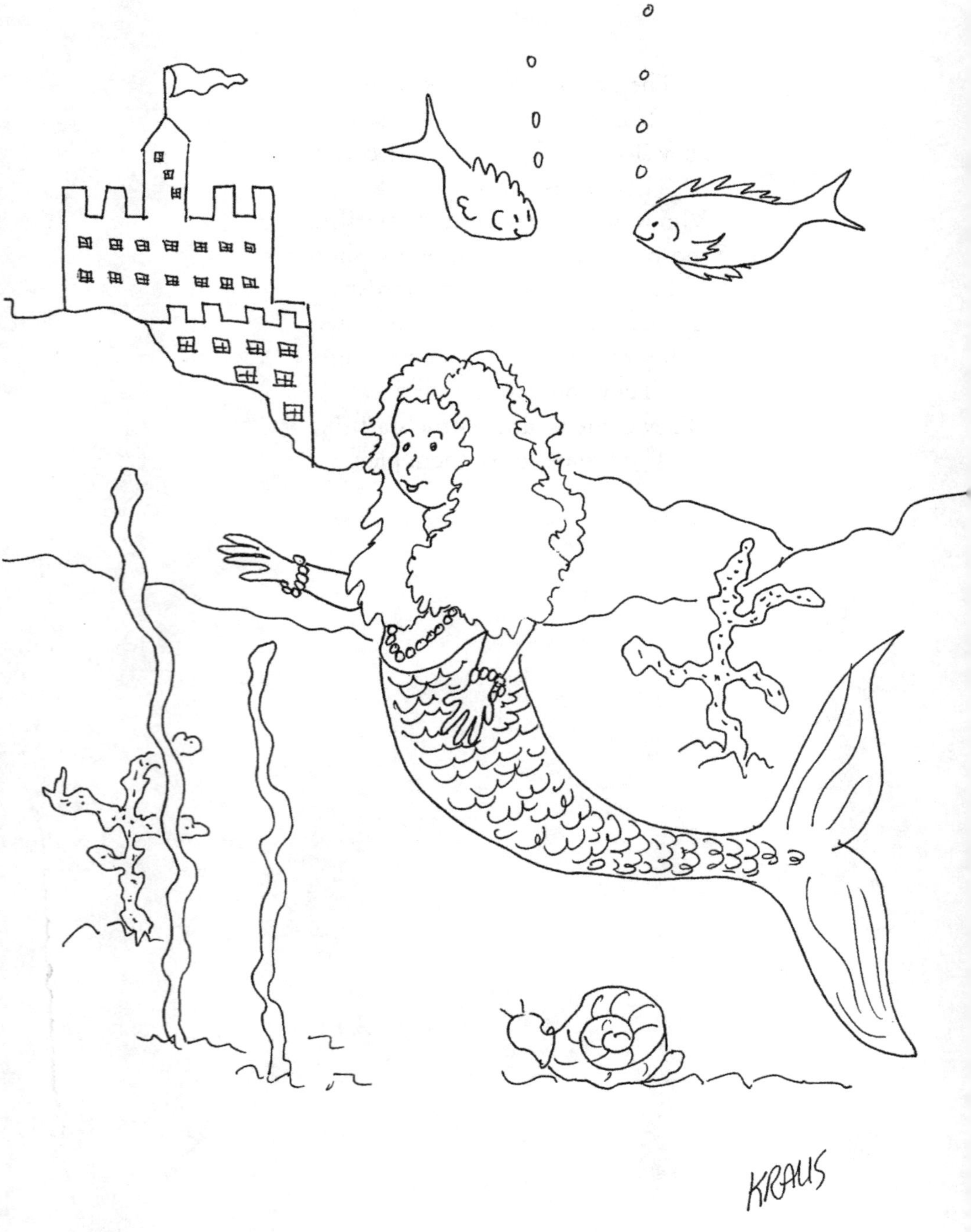
KRAUS

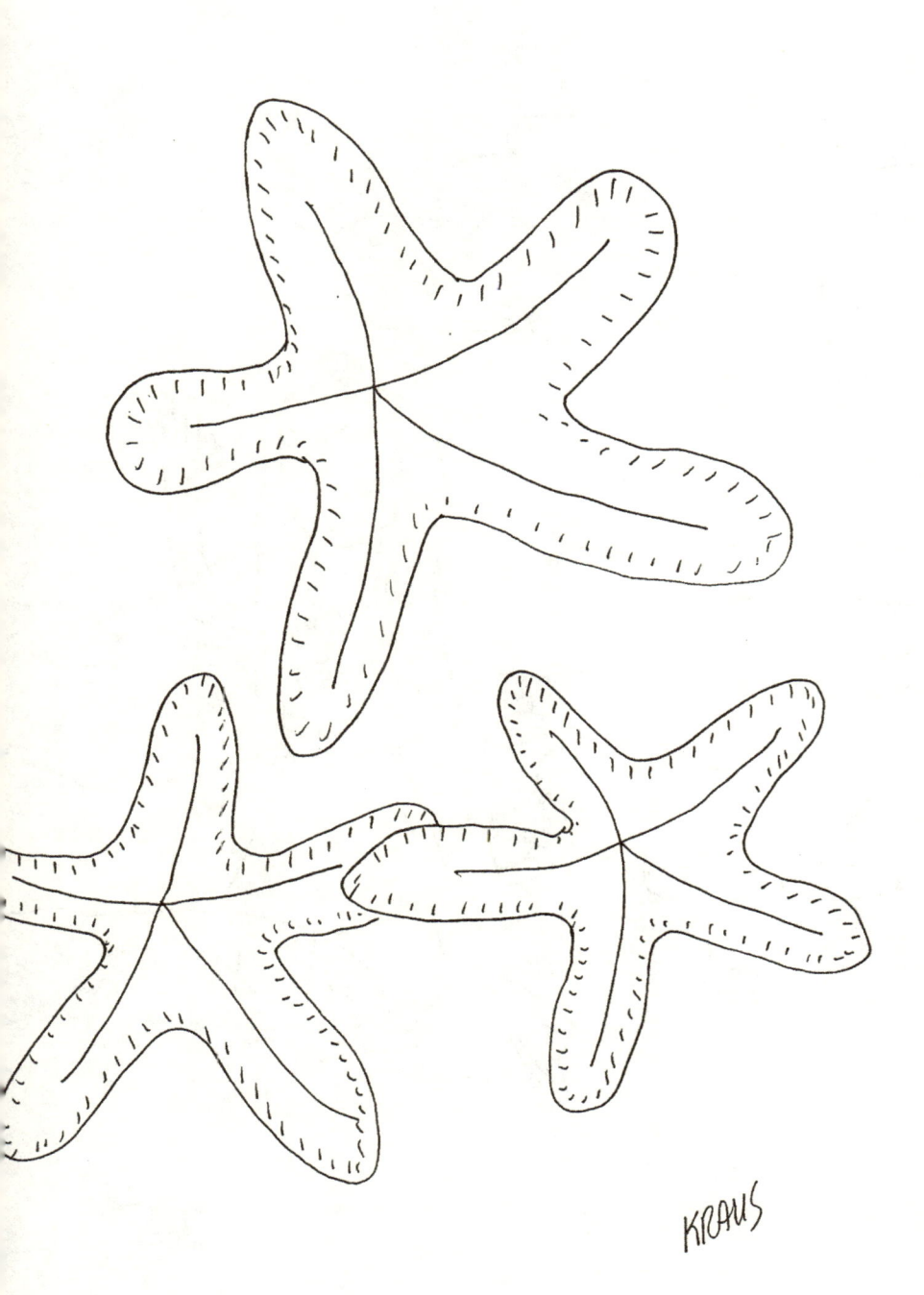

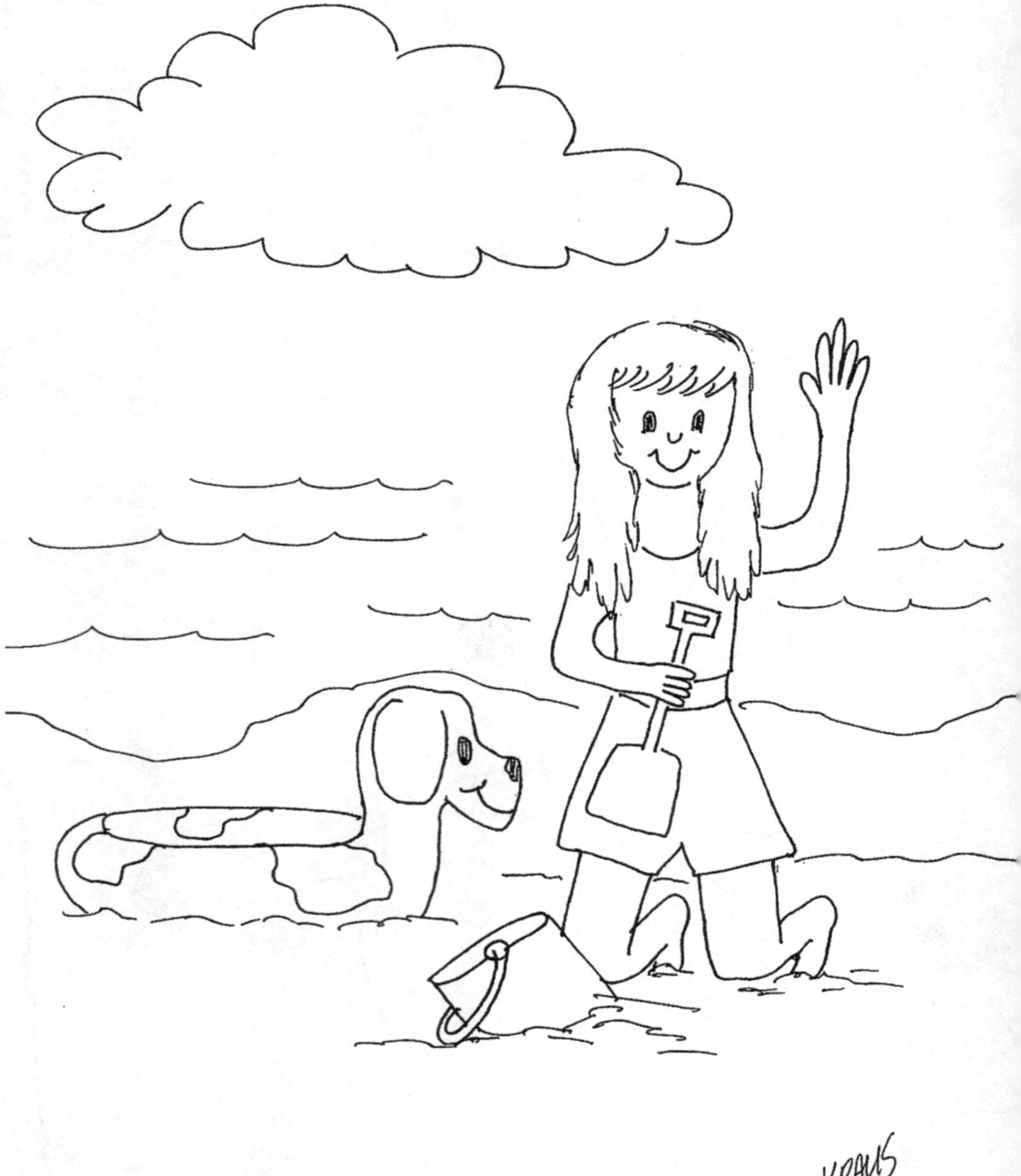
KRAUS

If You Should Go to the Zoo

The Visit to the Zoo

One hot day in summer,
When the sun was beaming down,
We went to the zoo
To see the animals of renown.

The elephants were very large
And seemed to lumber all about.
They liked to eat our peanuts;
One sniffed us with his snout.

Next on our list to see
Were polar bears at play.
They were romping on the ice,
Having fun in every way.

The gorilla was almost human
The way he looked at me.
His big brown eyes seemed to say,
"I'm the best you'll ever see!"

The giraffes arched their lovely necks,
Looking in all directions
As they patrolled their cage…
I'm glad we passed those inspections!

We loved it all, every wondrous thing we saw.
The seals, the parrots, the monkeys too.
There are such a lot of animals
That are entertained by visitors at the zoo!

    Have the child choose a favorite animal to draw. Look on the Internet or find a book about that animal. Write several facts about it in a journal.
    Discuss if any of the animals' characteristics are similar to people you know. Does the eagle look like Uncle Myron?

In the Country, on the Farm

Farmer Brown

Howdy! I'm Farmer Brown.
I live far away from town.
I have a lot of cows and sheep.
I hardly ever get to sleep.
I like to take my fishin' pole
And go down to the fishin' hole.
It's there that I get some rest
And watch a bluebird build its nest.
It took a while for me to know
That no matter where I go,
Whether I see something old or new,
It's not as good as what I do!
And so I'm very happy here.
Sometimes I even see a deer.
You come visit me some more.
Life on the farm is not a bore!

Sam, the Country Boy

Sam lives in the country.
He loves the outside air.
He likes to climb the fences.
He likes to run everywhere.
When the air is sunny and warm,
And the day is sunshine bright,
He can watch the cows and sheep,
And count the stars at night.
He sees the newborn baby colt
That likes to tease his mother.
He runs and kicks his heels,
But really, he's no bother.
Life on the farm is lots of fun.
It brings Sam lots of joy.
It's the place he wants to stay and later…
Raise his own little boy.

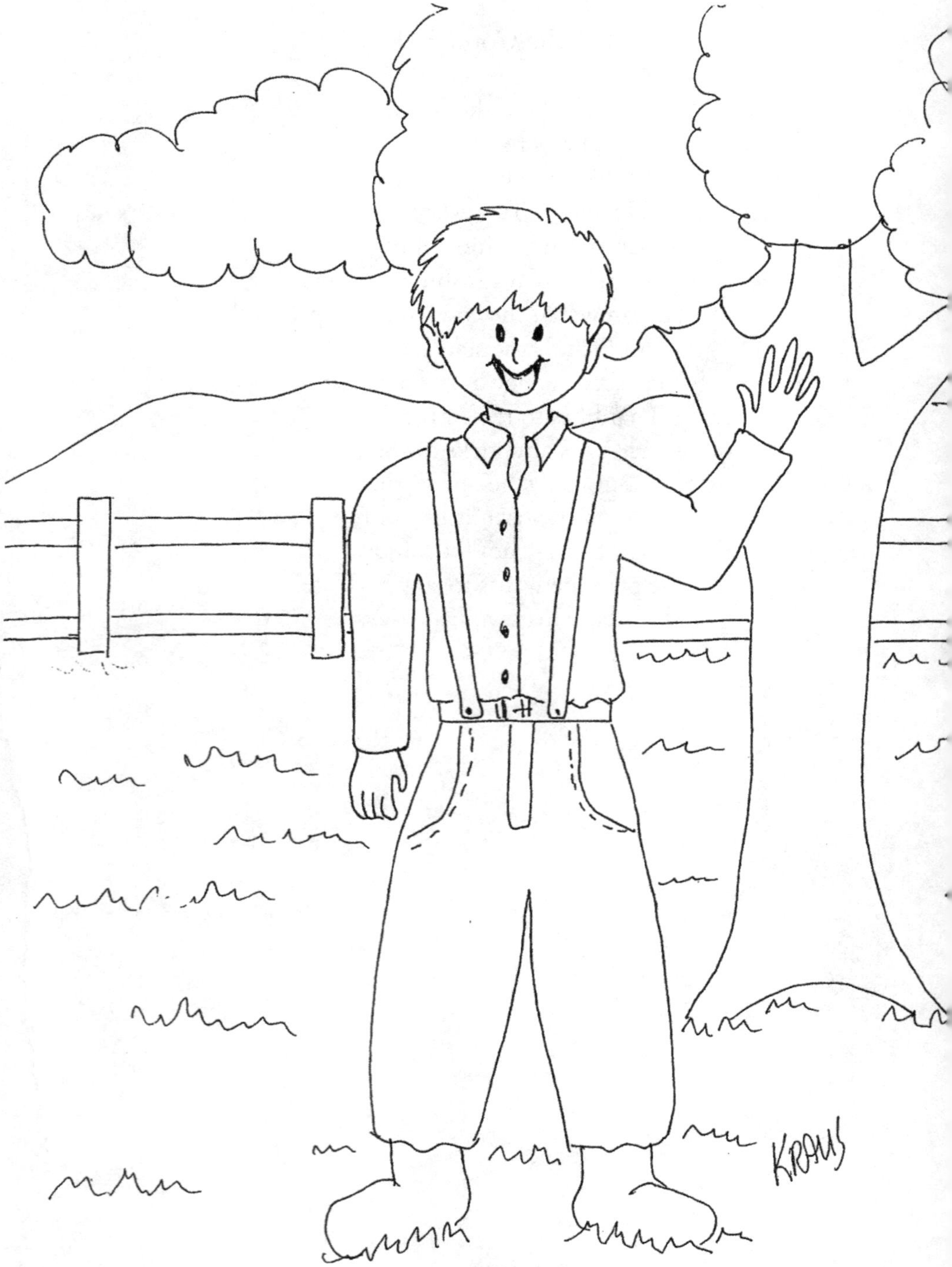

The Fourth of July

Be sure to explain this holiday. It's a vital part of our history.

Fireworks

The night for watching fireworks has arrived.
We were all excited to be going to town
To watch the fireworks and hear the BOOMING sounds.
It would be the best show around.

The cooler was packed with lots of cold drinks
And some sandwiches to eat.
The colors of the fireworks sure would be neat
And we could watch from a front row seat.

We set up our chairs in the very best place,
And settled down to watch the program begin.
It won't start until darkness sets in.
Then the first rocket takes off with a spin!

We saw flowers, rockets, and spirals of green.
The colors were grand and very bright!
We saw them explode with a fiery light!
Their brightness lit up the entire night!

All of this fun lasted about an hour.
Then it was time to go home to bed.

I laid down my sleepy head,
But I could still see in my mind's eye
Those colors of yellow, green, and red!

Fireworks Celebration

See the fireworks climb up high.
Hear them exploding in the sky.
See the fiery sparks float by.
I just look in awe and sigh.

218

Exploring the House

Treasure in the Attic

There's a treasure in the attic.
I found it yesterday.
I thought it was my greatest luck
To find this stuff, I say.
There were a lot of costume clothes
Packed in a trunk up there.
I opened up the battered chest.
And I began to stare.
There was a hat, a cane, and hair.
What a story it could tell!
Everyone who had used this stuff
Was gone. I knew that well.
I put on the hat and twirled the cane.
I made a silly rhyme.
Then I danced across the floor…
I had a real good time.

Fun in the Kitchen

There's an orchestra that hides in the kitchen.
Mr. Nobody plays the pots, and I Don't Know plays the pans.
They always leave their instruments lying on the floor.
Gee, I wish they'd let me play some more.

Under the Sofa

I looked under the sofa. I found a nickel and a dime.
This looking through the house wouldn't be a waste of time.
I looked under the cushions. I found popcorn and lots of dirt.
I looked under my bed, and, gee, I found my shirt!

222

The Circus Comes to Town

The Circus

The circus with its acrobats
And all the silly clowns
Turns my normal world
To smiles instead of frowns.

Yes, it's a happy place for me
To go and be amused.
I like to see the elephants,
And MAYBE…kangaroos!

The circus is like a world
Of wonder and fantasy.
The colors of the costumes
Are as bright as they can be.

It is a shame to leave this place
Of merriment and cheer,
But I can go home, knowing
It will come back next year.

Circus Clowns

The circus clowns act so silly!
How do they ever get that way?
They ride around in a little car
And pretend to have a fray.
Each one wears great big shoes
And sports a tricky bouquet.
They have crazy colored wigs to wear
And smiles that last all day!

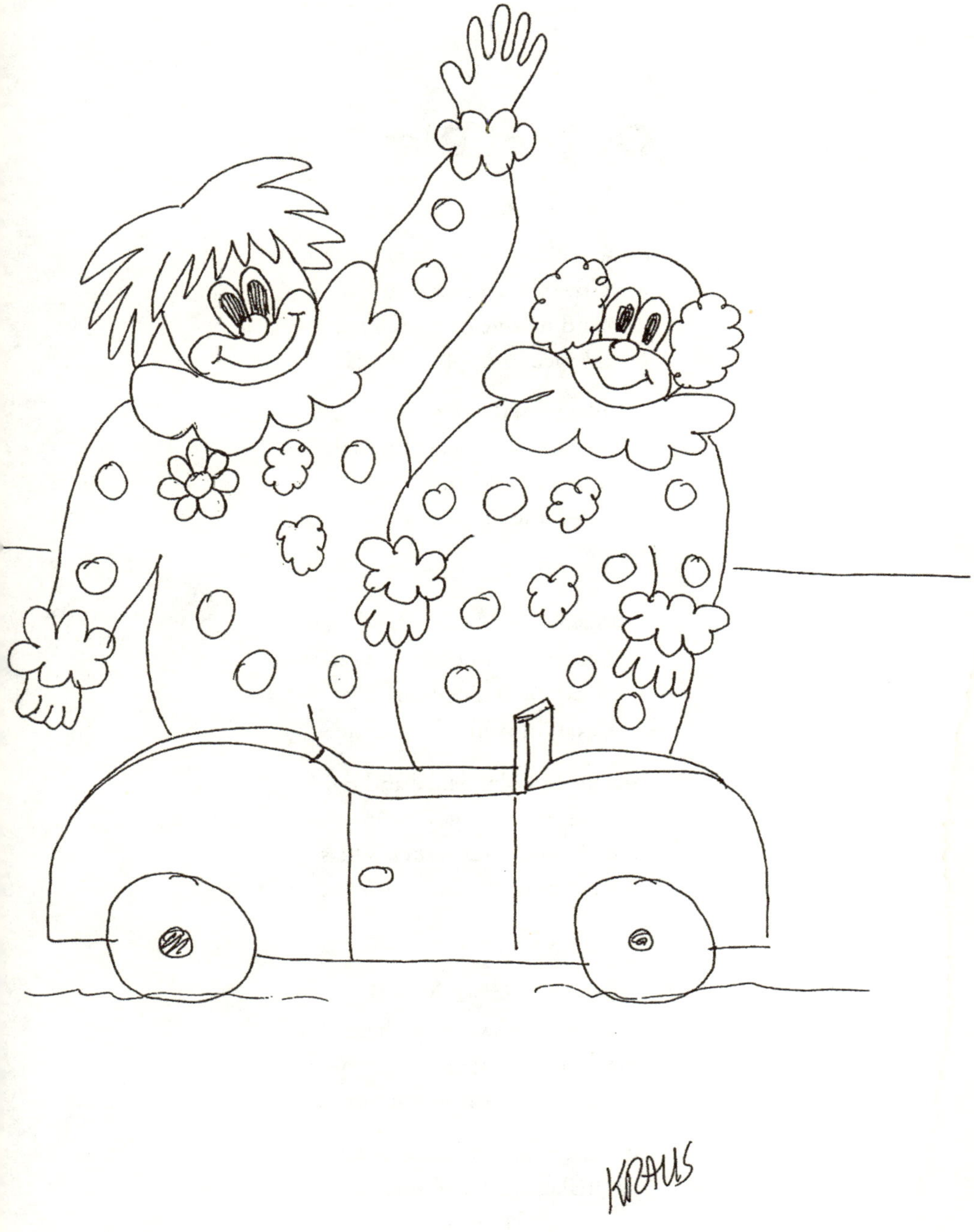
KRAUS

Or Just Playing

Skateboard

My skateboard is my favorite thing.
I love the wind in my face,
And no one can catch me
As I race from place to place!

I like to make my skateboard
Do flips and bounce it high!
Sometimes I think it will
Take me up into the sky!

Blowing Bubbles

Blowing bubbles is lots of fun.
See them shine in the sun!
I can blow them quickly.
Watch me! One. Two. Three!

See the bubbles dance and twirl.
See all the colors swirl.
Blowing bubbles is such a blast!
It's a shame this fun won't last.

Going to the Park

It's fun to go the park.
I love the swing set there.
Watch me swing so way up high;
The wind whips through my hair!

And the spiral slide is really cool!
It makes me laugh out loud!
Hmm,
Summer is sure more fun than school!

LEARNING LETTERS

A B C to X Y Z

Easy to say and easy to see!

A B C to X Y Z

A is for apple, ant, and add.

B is for boy, baker, and bad.

C is for cat, candle, and can.

D is for dog, dimple, and Dan.

E is for end, Ellie, and Ed.

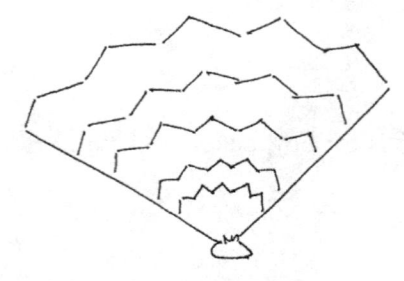

F is for fan, fiddle, and fed.

G is for girl, guy, and golly.

H is for hug, hello, and holly.

I is for imp, in, and colored inks.

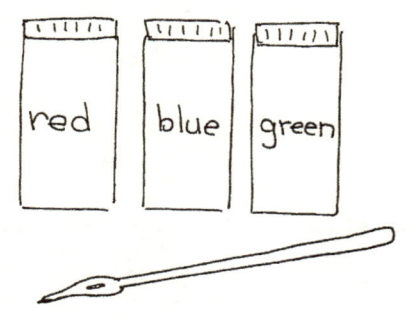

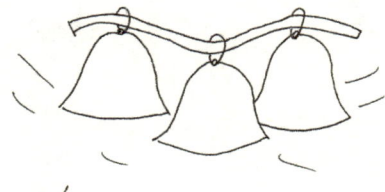

J is for jump, jingle, and jinx.

ding dong ding

K is for king, kangaroo, and kick.

L is for lion, lazy, and lick.

M is for man, morning, and map.

N is for no, naughty, and nap.

O is for on, often, and ox.

P is for put, puddle, and pox.

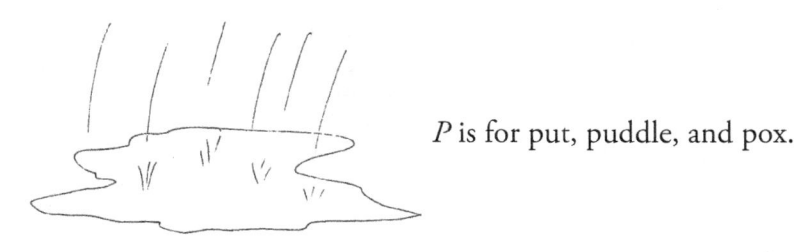

Q is for quick, quiet, and quack.

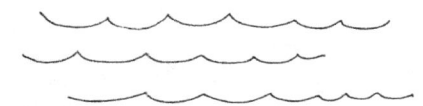

R is for race, river, and rack.

S is for sick, Sam, and sable.

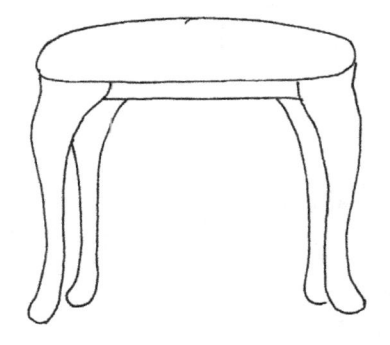

T is for Tom, token, and table.

U is for us, up, and undo.

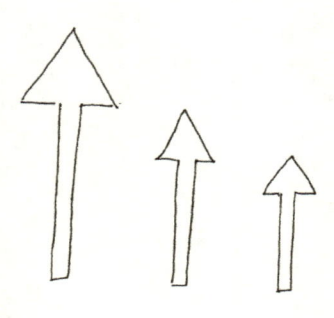

V is for vim, value, and view.

W is for wig, wagon, and way.

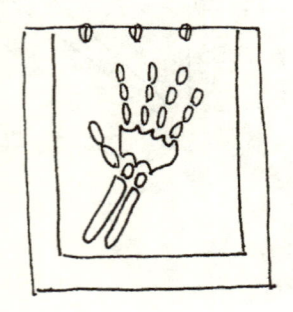

X is for Xerxes, xenia, and x-ray.

Y is for yes, yummy, and you.

Z is for zip, zebra, and zoo.

I've just said all the letters.
They're what I need to know
When I want to send a note
To say, "I love you so!"

Yes, it's letters I will use
To read and write each day.
These little letters are my friends
That help me along the way.

They open up the pages of my favorite storybooks.
They tell me about fairies and pirates with hooks.
Because I know the letters and say them one by one
I can open any book and have a lot of fun!

The Story of A B C to X Y Z

This alphabet story is to help the children learn the alphabet sequence. The children should draw a picture to match each part of the story.

Once upon a time, there was a little APPLE. APPLE lived in an A-frame house. APPLE was very happy in the house. One day, a bad BOY on a bike came to the A-frame house. The bad BOY took APPLE away.

The bad BOY rode away very fast with APPLE. He rode over CAT's tail. CAT meowed loudly.

CAT made such an awful noise that DOG was worried. DOG came out of his house to see if CAT was OKAY.

DOG barked for help for CAT. But DOG's barking didn't help CAT at all. ELEPHANT at the nearby zoo could hear both of them making awful noises. ELEPHANT listened with her big, big ears.

All of this excitement made for a very long day. ELEPHANT was tired. The zoo was closing. As the zoo closed, FIREWORKS shot into the air.

All the people who had come to see ELEPHANT were leaving the zoo. They watched the FIREWORKS as they went out the GATE.

They went HOME to go to sleep. All the people were happy to be HOME.

One of the people was INDIAN. INDIAN had been at the zoo, and now he was HOME. INDIAN was happy.

INDIAN put on his JAMMIES to go to sleep. He was glad to be in his own cozy bed.

INDIAN'S JAMMIES had little KANGAROOS on them.

The little brown KANGAROOS were eating LOLLIPOPS. The LOLLIPOPS were many different colors.

MONKEY was in a tree outside, watching through the window. He could see INDIAN in his JAMMIES with the KANGAROOS that were eating the LOLLIPOPS. MONKEY was busy watching.

While MONKEY was in the tree, he saw a NEST with eggs in it. It was a very big NEST.

The eggs in the NEST were OVAL eggs.

MONKEY discovered the NEST with the OVAL eggs. PEACOCKS were hatching from the OVAL eggs.

The PEACOCKS grew and grew into big lovely birds. They had beautiful feathers. QUEEN wanted their feathers.

QUEEN wanted their feathers to decorate her ROBE.

Her ROBE had S designs on it. QUEEN'S ROBE had Ss all over it. It was very pretty.

QUEEN decided to wear her ROBE with the Ss to the TEMPLE.

The day she went to the TEMPLE, it was raining. She needed her UMBRELLA.

Her UMBRELLA had VALENTINES on it.

She went to the TEMPLE. She carried her UMBRELLA with the VALENTINES on it. She WALKED all the way.

She WALKED home too.
And that was the end of her day.
And this is the end of the story.
It has to end this way.
She shouted, "X, Y, Z!
That's enough story for me!"

About the Author

Rebecca has a BA degree in elementary education followed by master's work in counseling and creative writing. She plied these skills and strategies in her thirty years' experience to introduce children to the wonders of learning.

Rebecca loves using pictures, which inspire the child's appreciation for art. She also enjoys participating in several sports. Her writing encourages the child to try a variety of experiences.

The world of young minds is full of imagination and a love for adventure. Enjoy traveling with your child on this adventure.

CPSIA information can be obtained
at www.ICGtesting.com
Printed in the USA
JSHW021144260123
36767JS00001B/13

9 781685 707644